WILSON AND THE LEAGUE OF NATIONS

WILSON AND THE LEAGUE OF NATIONS

Why America's Rejection?

Edited by RALPH A. STONE

Miami University

HOLT, RINEHART AND WINSTON
New York · Chicago · San Francisco · Toronto · London

Cover illustration: Woodrow Wilson on a speaking
tour. (Library of Congress)

CONTENTS

INTRODUCTION

The fight over the League of Nations from 1918 to 1920 is a dramatic and significant chapter in recent American history. The drama lies principally in the struggle's many conflicts—between personalities, ideas, institutions, political parties, and branches of government—and the significance in the impact of those conflicts on subsequent events and in the nature of the issues raised during the fight. Because scholars differ over the reasons for the League's defeat, because they cannot agree on the fight's significance, and because many of the issues are still relevant and unresolved, we have a problem worthy of consideration. This book of readings is about that problem.

It will be helpful to look first at the leading personality of the fight since he is at the center of so much of the controversy. The League of Nations and the name Woodrow Wilson will always be joined. Wilson made the League his greatest cause. He became an early convert to the idea of collective security and around it shaped many of his policies both before and during participation of the United States in World War I. After the war he represented the United States at the peace conference, where he succeeded in making the idea a reality and in getting the League incorporated as an integral part of the Treaty of Versailles. The Treaty was, of course, much more than just the League of Nations. Its articles concerning territorial divisions, reparations, and war guilt, to mention only three examples, aroused considerable debate in their own right. Certain immigrant groups disliked the articles that drew European boundaries not in keeping with the principle of self-determination. Liberals protested the violations of self-determination and the harshness of the terms for Germany. Wilson himself realized there were weaknesses in the Treaty, but he saw in the League, tied as it was to the rest of the Treaty, an instrument for rectifying some of the past mistakes and preventing future ones. Thus, his final effort: to persuade the American people and through them the Senate to approve the Treaty and thereby bring the United States into the League. In this he failed. His strenuous speaking tour around the nation proved futile. If fires were lighted in the hinterland, they failed to reach Washington with enough heat to affect senators. And the tour almost proved fatal when Wilson suffered a massive stroke. Shortly thereafter the Senate

1

rejected the Treaty, on three separate votes in November 1919, and finally in March 1920. If this was not the *coup de grâce*, the election in November 1920 of Warren G. Harding as president surely was. Wilson's crusade, which had begun on a high note of optimism, ended as a bitter and tragic failure.

Some writers see great irony in Wilson's failure. The League's most ardent champion, they point out, was also its worst enemy. Whether from his physical breakdown or from his single-minded determination to see the League approved, or from a combination of these and other causes, Wilson was unable to compromise. When it became apparent that the Senate would not accept the Treaty unless reservations were added, Wilson should have made concessions. Other writers, however, praise Wilson for the concessions he did make to his opponents and for not compromising further when to do so would have destroyed the substance of what he sought to achieve. Why Wilson refused to accept an accommodation and whether his decision was, in retrospect, a wise one are questions that go to the heart of the problem.

One man's tragedy is often another's triumph. If Woodrow Wilson comes first to mind when the League is mentioned, Henry Cabot Lodge follows close behind. The contest between these two protagonists colors almost every aspect of the fight. As Senate majority leader of the Republican party and chairman of the Foreign Relations Committee, Lodge held a position of power and responsibility second only to the president. At one time he had shown interest in a league, but by 1918 his interest had begun to wane. Whether his change of mind owed more to an intense dislike of Wilson as a man and to the Democrats as a party than to a sincere ideological antipathy to Wilson's version of collective security is a moot point. Separating a man's motives is at best a difficult task and in Lodge's case it might be impossible. Perhaps a more meaningful question would be: how well did the Massachusetts senator fulfill his duties as a responsible opposition leader? Involved here are related questions concerning the proper function of an opposition party and its leader and the meaning of bipartisanship in foreign affairs.

Wilson and Lodge merit close attention, but to understand why they acted as they did one must analyze the underlying and more impersonal forces at work. There were many such forces and, as in the case of personalities, writers do not always see eye to eye on their relative importance. Some historians, for example, have argued that the Constitution of the United States was the biggest obstacle to the League's acceptance. According to this view, it was the Constitution's separation of powers, especially its failure to define clearly the respective treaty-making powers of the President and Senate, which created suspicion and jealousy between the two branches, thus lessening the chance of an agreement. Aggravating this inherent difficulty was the resentment felt by many senators toward Wilson as a result of the wartime expansion of executive powers. Even more significant was the Congressional election of 1918 which gave both houses of Congress to the Republicans. Thereafter, with Republicans in control of the Senate but with Democrats still holding the executive branch, the Constitutional checks and balances would operate even more effectively to block the Treaty's approval.

Another and quite different interpretation assigns less weight to the Constitutional barrier than to the basic ideological differences between the opponents and supporters of the League. One can argue that the clash pitted isolationism, a deeply rooted tradition which drew strength from its association with the revered Founding Fathers and its long record of success in the nineteenth century, against internationalism, a newly planted policy which had yet to demonstrate its viability for the twentieth century. So strong was the isolationist tradition that, as suggested by one historian, it may not be amiss to say that men long dead who were isolationists in a past context—Washington, Jefferson, and Monroe were the most venerated—had as much to do with the League's defeat as some men very much alive in 1920. More recently, however, it has been asserted that the ideological division was not between isolationists and internationalists but between two or more species of internationalists.

One of the interpretations still most widely held attributes the League's defeat to the partisan political atmosphere of the time. There is no doubt that politics had "reconvened" with a vengeance in late 1918, though actually politics were never "adjourned" during the war as Wilson had requested. Both parties thought the League might have a crucial bearing on their political futures. Republicans, eager to follow up their Congressional victory by capturing the White House in 1920, feared that Wilson and the Democrats would take credit for the League's creation; but even greater was their fear that the League issue would split their own party and ruin their chances in 1920. Democrats, well aware that their victory in 1912 was due to the Roosevelt-Taft split, feared that Republicans would try to avert a repetition of that disaster by uniting on an anti-League policy or at least taking credit for "Republicanizing" the League with amendments and reservations. The fears of both were exaggerated but not unfounded.

Since the main battleground of the fight was the Senate, it is well to note that august body's structure as it affected the League's defeat. The Republican majority was only 49 to 47 (one seat reversed would have meant a tie, which Vice-President Marshall could have broken in the Democrats' favor), but it was enough to give the party solid control over the committees. The key Foreign Relations Committee, through which the Treaty must pass, numbered 10 Republicans and 7 Democrats, whereas a more accurate reflection of the overall membership ratio would have been 9 to 8. Another advantage of the majority party was Senate rule 37. That much criticized rule permitted a simple majority of senators, in this case almost all Republicans, to attach reservations to the Treaty that were unacceptable to Wilson, hence to almost all Democrats, without whose votes the Treaty could not obtain the final two-thirds approval. After the Treaty had been voted down decisively in November 1919, about half of the Democrats switched to support the Treaty with reservations. However, enough Democratic senators followed Wilson's advice so that when the final vote came in March 1920, these "loyal" Democrats, in concert with the irreconcilables (who had helped attach reservations), rejected the Treaty by 7 votes.

In searching for answers to the question of responsibility for the League's defeat, few writers have failed to point out lessons that the great debate offers to the student of American foreign policy and political institutions. Different generations have seen different lessons, just as they have found somewhat different answers to the question of responsibility. In the 1930s historians often stressed the political and Constitutional aspects of the struggle and what they could mean for the future; during World War II writers were inclined to place the blame for the breakdown of the peace setttlement on failure of the United States to join the League; in the 1950s and 1960s, from the perspective of a Cold War, the League fight seemed to have more meaning for what it revealed about American attitudes toward fundamental concepts of international relations. So in the readings here selected one sees not only the different analyses of the League controversy but also the pattern of shifting historiography.

In the opening selection George H. Haynes presents a summary of the fight within the framework of the Constitutional conflict between the Senate and the President. Each side in the struggle, states Haynes, and in particular the two protagonists, knew well the difficulties presented by the Constitution's separation of powers. Wilson had carefully studied the problem of treaty making in his writings as a historian and political scientist. Lodge knew from his long service in the Senate just what was involved. Yet instead of facilitating cooperation, this intimate awareness seemed to make each side more ready to use "extraordinary methods to bend the other to its will," more anxious to point out the other's failures to act in the proper spirit. Neither side tried sufficiently hard to overcome the inherent obstacles imposed by the system. There was not enough "loyalty to a common master," the United States as a whole.

The next four authors reject, either explicitly or implicitly, the Constitutional interpretation in favor of an ideological or political explanation. Roland N. Stromberg disagrees with those who doubt the loyalty or good intentions of the participants. "A sounder interpretation," he believes, "would be one that portrayed men of reasonably good will struggling to decipher the meaning of the League system and to reconcile it with legitimate national interest—and in the end finding themselves baffled." In analyzing the reaction to Article 10, the heart of the League, he has sympathy for Republicans who grappled with the ambiguities and confusions in Wilson's concept of collective security. By the same token he is severely critical of Wilson's failure to do more to clarify the nature of Article 10's obligations. He maintains that "It seems time to lay to rest the legend of Republican 'isolationism' in 1919" and that Republican internationalists, such as Roosevelt, Root, and Lodge, performed a service by exposing the "fuzziness" of Wilsonianism.

Stromberg's book, published in 1963, is concerned almost solely with ideology. Writing exactly thirty years earlier, W. Stull Holt focused on the politics of the League fight. Party politics killed the League, he asserts; politics were the major theme that blended together all the minor themes. His central point is that in voting on the Lodge reservations senators, with a few exceptions, followed party lines. Republicans supported the reservations; Democrats opposed them. There never was any agreement because each party, in particular the Republican party led by Lodge, wanted to discredit the other.

Selig Adler agrees with both Holt and Stromberg to a point. Politics were present, he grants, but politics do not explain the widespread disenchantment with collective security. The answer is to be found in ideological differences, but not the kind described by Stromberg. In Adler's view a coalition was emerging between 1917 and 1920 composed of liberals, immigrant groups, and "blatant nationalists." Differing on many issues, this coalition nevertheless united in opposition to the Treaty and helped provide the impetus to the isolationist resurgence of the 1920s and 1930s. The most important group were the nationalists, led by William E. Borah and some of his irreconcilable colleagues, in the Senate. Much more powerful than their numbers alone would indicate, the irreconcilables not only marshaled anti-League opinion around the country but also brought pressure on Lodge whenever he seemed about to yield to moderate Republican internationalists. Adler concedes that internationalists did have a voice within the party, but he contends that isolationists were in control, especially after the election of 1920. Is the disagreement between Adler and Stromberg partly semantic? If so, what criteria should be used to define isolationism, internationalism, nationalism, and other such abstractions?

A chapter from John Chalmers Vinson's book, *Referendum for Isolation*, concludes the group of selections on politics and ideology. Vinson, like Adler and Stromberg, stresses ideological causes in the League's defeat, but he has something unusual to say about the election of 1920. Most historians, however they view the League fight, have described the presidential contest between Warren G. Harding and James Cox as inconclusive in demonstrating much about the American people's attitude toward the great issue of the day. There were so many other campaign issues competing for attention and so much political doubletalk that the public was either confused or bored by the candidates' statements on the League. The election certainly was no "solemn referendum," as Wilson had said it should be; and Harding's victory, enormous as it was, constituted no mandate for the president-elect's funeral oration two days after the returns when he declared that the League was "now deceased." Vinson challenges this prevailing interpretation. While he admits that there was much confusion, he maintains that one fact stood out clearly: the people rejected Article 10 of the League. However much they favored the idea of a league, they did not want to assume the commitments and obligations they thought inhered in this Article. The campaign statements of both Harding and Cox, the opinion of the contemporary press, and the events of the next two decades are sufficient evidence for saying that the election was a referendum, a "referendum for isolation."

Let us now look more closely at the role of Wilson and Lodge within the context of the preceding selections. The student will want to consider what part personal antagonism played in their actions, if either made a sincere effort to compromise, whether each had an equal responsibility to compromise. These questions are taken up in the next group of readings, first by Thomas A. Bailey in a selection from *Woodrow Wilson and the Great Betrayal*. In this volume, published in 1945, and in the companion volume, *Woodrow Wilson and the Lost Peace*, which appeared a year earlier, Bailey broke new ground. While sympathetic to Wilson's goals, he rejected the generally accepted view that Wilson was less guilty than Lodge for the League's defeat. Lodge certainly was not blameless, Bailey says, but his errors were not as serious as Wilson's. The magnitude of their culpability was proportionate to their responsibility for getting the Treaty passed. Wilson as leader of all of the people had a greater responsibility than did Lodge as leader of a party. Wilson should have compromised. He should have accepted the Lodge reservations, which did not, as he believed, emasculate the Treaty. Better yet he should not have put himself in the position of having to accept the Treaty with the Lodge reservations or of rejecting the whole; he could have avoided this position by cooperating with the mild reservationists. Why did he refuse to compromise? Why was there, ultimately, a failure of leadership? Bailey offers a variety of reasons: his principles, conception of duty, Scotch-Irish blood, hatred of Lodge, pride, sickness. The next two essays try to pinpoint the answer.

Alexander L. and Juliette L. George, a husband and wife team, have made an intensive personality study of Wilson. Their thesis is that he, having experienced "crushing feelings of inadequacy" as a child, sought to attain political power and to exercise that power in such a way as to compensate for his early "failures." These internal pressures which were the source of his strength were also the cause of his undoing; they "crippled his capacity to react objectively to matters at hand." When Lodge challenged the League of Nations, which was the quintessence of Wilson's effort to prove his worthiness (as a man even more than as a politician), Wilson reacted blindly. He was driven irrationally into making the ill-fated "swing around the circle" instead of searching for a compromise. It was Wilson's personality weaknesses, understood and cleverly exploited by Lodge, that caused the defeat of the League.

Perry Laukhuff, by contrast, stresses the physical as opposed to the psychical causes of Wilson's failure. It was not megalomania, he states, or any other personality defect that primarily explains the lack of leadership. Rather, it was his physical breakdown on the Western trip. At the crucial point in the fight Wilson fell, sick and disabled. Out of touch with key advisers, deprived of his power of eloquence, unable to consult personally with senators, he simply could not give the brilliant leadership he had shown in the past. If Wilson was "emotionally unable" at this time to lead, as Laukhuff concedes at the end of his article, it was due to his paralyzing stroke. A physically healthy president, he concludes, would have carried the United States into the League.

The interpretations of Bailey and the Georges picture Wilson as extremely uncompromising. A recent article by Kurt Wimer undertakes to disprove this charge by showing that Wilson, during the critical months of July and August of 1919, did try to reach an agreement with the Senate. Wimer believes that Wilson's individual conferences with Republican senators and his proposed "adjustment" on the matter of reservations to the Treaty represent a serious effort at conciliation and even compromise. Does Wimer's evidence support his conclusions? Was Wilson's "adjustment" realistically designed to win over the Republican mild reservationists or was it a way to force Lodge and his followers into the same position in which the Democrats had been placed by Lodge? Were the mild reservationists under Lodge's control, as Wimer implies? These questions suggest that the key to the parliamentary struggle in the Senate lay within the Republican party. Thus we come to the role of Lodge, which is discussed in the next group of readings.

To Woodrow Wilson's supporters, Henry Cabot Lodge has often been the villain of the piece. This hostile view is presented by Denna Frank Fleming, who might be considered the dean of historians of the League fight. His was the first full-length treatment, and until Bailey's books appeared it received no serious challenge. Its influence is apparent in the books by Holt and Haynes. An ardent champion of collective security, Fleming has few kind words for those who question Wilson's ideas. He recognizes that Wilson made certain tactical mistakes, but he leaves no doubt that it is Lodge, not Wilson, who deserves censure.

One of Lodge's persistent defenders has been his grandson, Henry Cabot Lodge, Jr., himself once a senator and, perhaps ironically, ambassador to the United Nations under Eisenhower. In John Garraty's biography of the elder Lodge, the grandson offers his comments. Garraty, utilizing manuscript sources hitherto unavailable, finds Lodge guilty of partisanship, pettiness, and hatred; but his biggest failing was his refusal "to assume any responsibility." While admitting the desirability of a league, he refused to do anything positive toward creating one that was "workable." Lodge, Jr., disputes these criticisms and argues that his grandfather's reservations prove he was a responsible, constructive critic. His closing remarks draw comparisons between the League and the United Nations. One among many pregnant questions raised by this selection is: what was—and is—a "workable" system of collective security?

And today? Has Wilson's vision now been vindicated? The final group of selections addresses this question. William G. Carleton opens the debate with a ringing affirmative. Wilson deserves to be ranked among the three greatest presidents, Carleton states, and "if rated solely on the basis of long-range impact on international relations, Wilson is the most influential of all. . . ." Only carping critics whose standards for judging Wilson are higher than for judging other similar figures have prevented his reputation from soaring to its rightful niche. Wilson was a true realist in foreign policy: he combined the balance of power with collective security, realizing that the latter would gradually replace the former. Today, the long-time policy of the United States is still a Wilsonian policy. Wilson's solutions are more prophetic and urgent than ever.

Robert E. Osgood is similarly concerned with Wilson's place in history, but his concern is not that Wilson's reputation has been unfairly lowered but that it has been raised by naïve admirers who fail to understand the distinction between what Wilson preached and today's statesmen practice. Wilson's conception of collective security, Osgood writes, is not being practiced today by American statesmen. Neither in organizations such as NATO nor even in the United Nations have his ideas become reality. Rather than depending upon universal obligations of a legal and moral nature, policy makers have rightly acted from considerations of power and self-interest. Yet the Wilsonian ideal has been so strong that Americans still talk—and to some extent think—in the language of universal law and morality. The obvious danger is in confusing myth with reality. By viewing Wilson in the proper perspective, Osgood concludes, we can improve our own vision of the world.

It is fitting that Arthur S. Link, Wilson's eminent biographer, should have the last word. Link's position is somewhere between Carleton and Osgood: he praises Wilson's concept of collective security, arguing that the occurrence of World War II was due not to the fault of the League but to the failure of people to meet their responsibilities; at the same time he admits that only regional organizations such as NATO, the kind Wilson denounced, have been at all promising as security systems. Whether Wilson's ideas and ideals will ever be realized only the future can tell. "One thing," however, "is certain, now that men have the power to sear virtually the entire face of the earth: The prophet of 1919 was right in his larger vision; the challenge that he raised then is today no less real and no less urgent than it was in his own time."

It is on this note of challenge that the readings end. There are, it is clear, many interpretations of who or what killed the League of Nations, just as there are many lessons to be drawn from its defeat. The interpretations often clash, but they sometimes complement one another; the same is true of the lessons. In wrestling with the interpretations, the student will face the complexities that confront anyone who examines the past. In comparing the lessons, he may come to appreciate the statesman's task of *having* to learn from history. In attempting to reach his own answers for his own generation, he will rely not only upon his knowledge of the past but also upon his understanding of the present and his vision of the future.

In the reprinted selections footnotes appearing in the original sources have in general been omitted unless they contribute to the argument or better understanding of the selection.

The Controversy in Brief

Party Politics Killed the League

"Throughout the entire proceedings runs the theme of party politics. . . . It can be asserted with as much certainty as is possible in human affairs that a sincere belief based on the merits of the issue was not the dominant cause of the Senate's action."—W. Stull Holt, *Treaties Defeated by the Senate* (Baltimore, 1933).

Article 10 Was the Stumbling Block

"Article 10 was the stumbling block that prevented attachment to the League. The ensuing long and bitter debate over its meaning was often obscure, yet none the less real. Men *felt* that a vital issue was involved."—Roland N. Stromberg, *Collective Security and American Foreign Policy, From the League of Nations to NATO* (New York, 1963).

The Constitution Was to Blame

"For this whole fateful series of events history is likely to place the chief blame upon the Constitution. . . ."—Charles P. Howland, *Survey of American Foreign Relations 1928* (New Haven, Conn., 1928).

Wilson's Illness Was Responsible

"Woodrow Wilson's physical disability deprived the country of leadership, the lack of leadership kept us out of the League of Nations, and quite possibly our absence from the League made possible the Second World War."—Perry Laukhuff, "The Price of Woodrow Wilson's Illness" [*The Virginia Quarterly Review*, XXXII (Autumn, 1956)].

Lodge's View of Wilson and Lodge's Biographer's View of Lodge

"It was killed by Wilson. He has been the marplot from the beginning. All the delays and all the troubles have been made by him. . . ."—Henry Cabot Lodge to Elihu Root, December 3, 1919, as quoted in John A. Garraty, *Henry Cabot Lodge, A Biography* (New York, 1953).

"To Henry Cabot Lodge the success of the Republican Party was of paramount importance. . . . In the last analysis, Lodge preferred a dead league to the one proposed by Wilson."—John A. Garraty, *Henry Cabot Lodge, A Biography* (New York, 1953).

The People's Verdict

"One of the most enduring myths in American history is that the election of 1920 was a solemn mandate from the American people to have no traffic with the League of Nations."—Thomas A. Bailey, *Woodrow Wilson and the Great Betrayal* (New York, 1945).

"In retrospect it is clear that America's final rejection of Article Ten, as well as the balance of the League of Nations Covenant, came November 2, 1920, with the landslide of Harding to the Presidency. . . . The people concurred in this judgment." John Chalmers Vinson, *Referendum for Isolation, Defeat of Article Ten of the League of Nations Covenant* (Athens, Ga., 1961).

Woodrow Wilson and Today's World

". . . a faithful interpretation of Wilson's view of an association of nations reveals how poorly his conception of collective security fits contemporary American practice and how badly the prevailing American conception of collective security is distorted by the efforts to reconcile the two."—Robert E. Osgood, "Woodrow Wilson, Collective Security, and the Lessons of History" [*Confluence*,V (Winter, 1957)].

". . . the chief claim of Wilson to a superlative place in history . . . is that he, more than any other, formulated and articulated the ideology which was the polestar of the Western democracies in World War I, in World War II, and in the decades of Cold War against the Communists."—William G. Carleton, "A New Look at Woodrow Wilson" [*The Virginia Quarterly Review*, XXXVIII (Autumn, 1962)].

The Constitutional interpretation is an old one. According to this view, the League was defeated principally because of executive-legislative jealousy, suspicion, and hostility arising from the Constitution's separation of powers, exacerbated by the forced cooperation of the two branches during the war and by the presence of strong-willed leaders on both sides. It was advanced as early as 1919–1920 and it continues to have its adherents. In this selection GEORGE H. HAYNES (1866–1947), for fifty years professor of economics and government at Worcester Polytechnic Institute and the author of many books and articles on representation, suffrage, and the initiative and referendum, as well as a two-volume study of the Senate, from which this selection is taken, emphasizes the Constitutional obstacles that blocked the League's acceptance. His interpretation should be compared especially with W. Stull Holt's, whose similar approach results in somewhat different conclusions.*

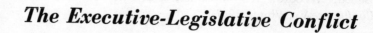

The Executive-Legislative Conflict

The unique conditions which the Senate's constitutional powers impose upon treaty-making between the United States and other nations are strikingly illustrated in the history of Senate action upon some treaties negotiated for the settlement of critical international issues at the end of the World War. In no other period have the questions at stake been so momentous and in none have the Executive and the Senate each used such extraordinary methods to bend the other to its will.

Breaking the precedent of six score years, President Wilson appeared in person before the Senate, January 22, 1917, to make a communication concerning the country's foreign relations. He stated his purpose as follows:

I have sought this opportunity to address you because I thought that I owed it to you, as the council associated with me in the final determination of our international obligations, to disclose to you without reserve the thought and purpose that have been taking form in my mind in regard to the duty of our Government in the days to come, when it will be necessary to lay afresh and upon a new plan the foundation of peace among the nations. . . . This Government should frankly formulate the conditions upon which it would feel justified in asking our people to approve its formal and solemn adherence to a League for Peace. . . . No covenant of co-operative peace that does not include the

* From George H. Haynes, *The Senate of the United States, Its History and Practice* (Boston: Houghton Mifflin Company, 1938), vol. 2, pp. 694–703, 713–718. Footnotes omitted.

peoples of the New World can suffice to keep the future safe against war. . . . There is no entangling alliance in a concert of power.

It is not necessary here to set forth the program which he then presented. The point to be noted is that nearly three months before the United States even entered the war, President Wilson felt it his duty to disclose to the Senate his thought and purpose as to this country's taking its place in a League for Peace. January 8, 1918, in an address before Congress he enunciated the "fourteen points" which it seemed to him should be considered as essentials in ending the conflict, and these and the principles set forth in two later addresses were put forward by the Germans in asking for an armistice, and were accepted with qualifications by the Allies as a basis for negotiation. It was because of this tentative acceptance of proposals which he himself had framed that President Wilson felt it his duty to go to Paris to take part in the peace negotiations. In announcing this determination at the opening session of Congress, December 2, 1918, he assured his hearers: "I shall be in close touch with you, . . . and you will know all that I do." Two days later he sailed for France.

A fortnight before the Armistice was signed, on the eve of the national election President Wilson had appealed thus to his countrymen:

If you have approved of my leadership and wish me to continue to be your unembarrassed spokesman in affairs at home and abroad, I earnestly beg that you will express yourselves unmistakably to that effect by returning a Democratic majority to both Senate and the House.

The response from the country should have disillusioned him, for the election returns showed that the new Senate, which would pass upon the treaty to be negotiated at Paris, would be controlled by a Republican majority, a result which he himself had said would be interpreted abroad as a repudiation of his leadership. Moreover, despite the theoretical objections that had repeatedly been urged against the service of Senators on peace missions, there was evident resentment among the Senators that none from their number had been included in the group of men—not submitted to the Senate for confirmation—whom the President had named as his colleagues.

He sailed for France, therefore, knowing that the Senate was to be controlled by the Republicans, that in its new organization the chairmanship of its dominant Committee on Foreign Relations would doubtless go to Senator Lodge than whom no one in the country stood more jealously for the Senate's constitutional share in the "making" of treaties, and that there was grave dissatisfaction with the makeup of the Peace Mission, because it included no member of the Senate, no representative member of the party which was to control the Senate, and no other American who in the mind of the people was of commanding eminence.

In the early weeks of the Congress little was heard of what was being done at Paris, but the most influential Senate leaders at once made plain their belief that a distinct and separate Treaty of Peace should first be made and that the formulation of a Covenant for a League of Nations should be postponed to a later time when its problems could be studied more dispassionately.

February 14, 1919, on the morning of the day when President Wilson was to read to a plenary session of the Peace Conference the newly completed draft of what he called "a constitution for a League of Nations," he cabled from Paris to Washington an invitation to the members of the Senate Committee on Foreign Relations and the House Committee on Foreign Affairs to dine with him at the White House; and to each of his thirty or more prospective guests he sent the message:

Each article [of this Covenant of the League of Nations] was passed only after a most careful examination by each member of the committee. There is a good and sufficient reason for the phraseology and substance of each article. I request that I be permitted to go over with you, article by article, the constitution before this part of the work of the Conference is made the subject of debate of Congress.

The discussions at that dinner conference, February 26, were confidential, but it is evident that the President made few, if any, converts to his program, and that old antagonisms were deepened.

In the closing hours of the Sixty-Fifth Congress, March 3, 1919, Lodge offered the following resolutions:

Whereas under the Constitution it is a function of the Senate to advise and consent to, or dissent from, the ratification of any treaty of the United States, and no such treaty can become operative without the consent of the Senate expressed by the affirmative vote of two-thirds of the Senators present; and . . .
Whereas a committee of the Conference has proposed a constitution for a league of nations, and the proposal is now before the Peace Conference for its consideration: Now, therefore, be it
Resolved by the Senate of the United States in the discharge of its Constitutional duty in regard to treaties, That it is the sense of the Senate that, while it is their sincere desire that the Nations of the World should unite to promote peace and general disarmament, the constitution of the league of nations in the form now proposed to the Peace Conference should not be accepted by the United States; and be it
Resolved further, That it is the sense of

the Senate that the negotiations on the part of the United States should immediately be directed with the utmost expedition to the urgent business of negotiating peace terms with Germany satisfactory, to the United States and the nations with whom the United States is associated in the war against the German Government, and that the proposal for a League of Nations to insure the peace of the world should be then taken up for careful and serious consideration.

Consideration of these resolutions was at once blocked, but at Lodge's request they were inserted in the *Record* together with the names of thirty-seven men, Senators and Senators-elect of the Sixty-Sixth Congress, who declared that, had they had the opportunity, they would have voted for these resolutions. By this famous "round-robin" formal notice was served on the President that this group of Senators utterly disapproved of the feature of the peace settlement which he had most at heart, that they urged the relegation of the League of Nations to the background, and that they held at least four more votes than were needed to defeat any treaty proposal which he might lay before the Senate. Never before nor since in the history of American treaty-making have Senators asserted such a dictatorial attitude while a treaty was in process of being negotiated.

The President's response was immediate and defiant. Addressing a great audience at the New York Metropolitan Opera House the day after this senatorial warning had been given, he declared that when he returned from Paris so many threads of the treaty would be "tied to the covenant that you cannot dissect the covenant from the treaty without destroying the whole vital structure." On the morrow he again sailed for France.

The contrast between the tone of President Wilson's response to the Senators' warning note and that of the British Prime Minister to a similar indication of opposition in Parliament was strikingly shown, a month later. April 8, a telegram was sent from three hundred and seventy members of Parliament demanding "Mr. Lloyd George's adhesion to his election pledges." "Public opinion indeed necessitated the return of the Prime Minister to England on the 14th of April to speak in the House." The very next day after the sending of this British counterpart to the Senators' "round-robin" came the Prime Minister's reply, that he would keep his pledges; and on the 15th of April he spoke in the House of Commons, explaining his course.

April 29, two days after the publication of the official text of the treaty, Lodge, and Curtis, the Republican whip, feeling certain that a special session of Congress would soon be called, sent telegrams to their Republican colleagues requesting that they "reserve final expressions of opinion respecting the amended League Covenant . . . until there had been opportunity for conference." This was equivalent to official notice of an intent to deal with the treaty as a party measure.

When Congress convened, May 19, after a recess of ten weeks, the Republicans, with a majority of two, assumed control with Lodge as majority leader. July 10, 1919, President Wilson appeared before the Senate, and presented the treaty with an eloquent appeal for its acceptance. He declared:

> My services and all the information I possess will be at your disposal and at the disposal of the Committee on Foreign Relations at any time, either informally or in session, as you may prefer; and I hope that you will not hesitate to make use of them.

At the end of his address, it was at once ordered that the injunction of secrecy upon the treaty be removed, and that the treaty be referred to the Committee on Foreign Relations.

In the reorganization of the Senate there had been given to this committee a membership of ten Republicans and seven Democrats, reversing the party allotment in the previous Congress. Of its personnel Lodge wrote: "It will be seen at once that this was a strong committee and such as the existing conditions demanded." His interpretation of what "the existing conditions demanded" seemed sufficiently obvious. The minority leader bluntly declared in Senate debate that the committee had been packed with men "practically pledged to oppose the League of Nations," and John Sharp Williams made the same charge. Ex-President Taft's comment was to the same effect. Four Republicans were added to that party's representation on the committee. The coveted assignments to this premier committee of the Senate are by tradition given to men of comparatively long and distinguished service. Of the four who now became Lodge's colleagues not one had completed a single term: Harding had served four years; New and Johnson, two; while Moses had been a member of the Senate only four months; but every one of the four was clearly to be recognized as an irreconcilable opponent of the League. . . .

September 10, from the Committee on Foreign Relations, Lodge presented its report in the Senate recommending ratification with at least forty-five textual amendments, and four reservations. Within the next few days there were filed the views of the minority (the Democratic members of the committee) and the views of Senator McCumber, Republican, in disagreement with the majority report.

September 3, a week before Lodge's cynically hostile report had been placed before the Senate, President Wilson started on a trip to the Pacific coast, with the avowed purpose of appealing to the people of the country in support of the treaty then pending in the Senate—another utterly unprecedented step in American treaty-making. In the course of three weeks he traveled ten thousand miles and made impassioned pleas to great audiences in nearly thirty cities in states of the Far West. But he broke under the strain, and before the end of the month he was back in the White House, his days of leadership at an end.

For weeks the struggle continued. By the end of October the Senate had defeated all the amendments which the committee had presented. Late in the evening of the last day of the session, November 19, 1919, the vote came upon the Lodge resolution of consent to ratification, and with the fourteen reservations previously approved.[1] Earlier in the day the minority leader had presented in the Senate a letter from the President, declaring that in his opinion the resolution as it stood did not provide for ratification, but rather for the nullification of the treaty, and his hope that all true friends of the treaty would refuse to support that resolution. The first vote stood 39 yeas to 55 nays. Reconsidered, the second vote stood 41 yeas to 51 nays. A vote was then taken on a resolution for the treaty's unconditional ratification, and was rejected by a vote of 38 to 53.

But the issue would not down. December 13, Underwood urged that renewed effort be directed to find some basis of compromise. January 30 there were made public the efforts of an informal bipartisan commission, a group of four Republicans and five Democrats of the

[1] See p. 28.

Senate, who for a fortnight, without avail, had sought to find some modification of the Lodge reservations that would make possible the ratification of the treaty.

February 9, Lodge himself made the motion that brought the treaty again before the Senate. Hitchcock inserted in the *Record* a letter from the President stating certain reservations that were acceptable to him. Ten days before the final vote was taken, Hitchcock placed before the Senate the stricken President's uncompromising statement that in his opinion every one of the so-called reservations was "in effect a rather sweeping nullification of the treaty." He added: "I hear of reservationists and mild reservationists, but I cannot understand the difference between a nullifier and a mild nullifier."

March 19, 1920, upon the resolution to consent to the ratification of the treaty with fifteen reservations its advocates mustered a large majority, but it lacked seven votes of the constitutional requirement of two-thirds.

The President's treaty thus having been defeated, Congress tried its own hand at peace-making. The first joint resolution, "declaring peace," was vetoed by President Wilson on the ground that it did not seek to accomplish any of the objects for which this country had entered the war. A new resolution, presented from the Committee on Foreign Relations and sponsored by a former Secretary of State, Knox, after much debate and amending in each branch, was finally passed by small votes and signed by President Harding, July 2, 1921. . . .

In treaty-making the Constitution of the United States has associated the President and the Senate in positions of such independence that constant friction and frequent deadlocks are inevitable, unless they each recognize that loyalty to a common master constrains them to act together in courtesy and comity to gain for their country, not only security, but that position of moral leadership among the nations to which her people believe her entitled. It should be a matter, not of encroachment, but of co-operation. . . .

No man has ever laid greater stress upon the desirability of co-operation in treaty-making than did Woodrow Wilson. In a study of *Constitutional Government in the United States*, published only two years before he became President, upon this point he said:

> The policy which has made rivals of the President and Senate has shown itself in the President as often as in the Senate, and if the Constitution did indeed intend that the Senate should in such matters be an executive council, it is not only the privilege of the President to treat it as such, it is also his best policy and his plain duty. As it is now, the President and the Senate are apt to deal with each other with the formality and punctilio of powers united by no common tie except the vague common tie of public interest, but it is within their choice to change the whole temper of affairs in such matters and to exhibit the true spirit of the Constitution by coming into intimate relations of mutual confidence, by a change of attitude which can perhaps be effected more easily upon the initiative of the President than upon the initiative of the Senate.

How far President Wilson's practice in treaty-making came to differ from his earlier theory and intent, the world knows. As to the Treaty of Versailles, his explanation doubtless would have been that the circumstances of its negotiation with the plenipotentiaries of many other powers put it out of the range of ordinary treaties, and made impossible continuous "confidential communication while his plans were in course." Nevertheless, it is to be remembered that as soon as the draft of the League of Nations Covenant was completed at Paris—before it had even been read to a plenary session of the Conference—he arranged by cable an opportunity to discuss it clause by clause with the Senate and House Committees which had to do with foreign affairs, and that later in submitting the actual treaty to the Senate he expressed the hope that the Senate or its Committee on Foreign Relations would not hesitate to make use of his services and all the information he possessed. Yet, before the President and the Committee on Foreign Relations came together in informal conference, there had intervened nearly seven weeks. During this time, "while a great number of witnesses were called for the purpose of condemning or criticizing the treaty, no witnesses were called and no testimony sought to elucidate or explain the great purpose of international co-operation to prevent war."

This uncordial attitude toward the advances made by the President was not due merely to pique at his having failed to keep the Senate in touch with the negotiations, nor to disapproval of the treaty which had been negotiated. It was due also in considerable degree to the Senate's traditional stiffness and jealousy in insisting upon exercising an entirely independent judgment upon foreign relations and putting its individual stamp upon every important treaty that is made. Many years before, on the floor of the Senate, in referring to that part of a standing rule of the Senate which still makes provision for the formalities to be observed when the President meets with the Senate for the consideration of executive business, Senator Lodge had said: "Yet I think we should be disposed to resent it, if a request of that sort was made to us by the President"; and in the same debate he had cited with approval President Madison's refusal to meet with a committee of the Senate on the ground that in the making of appointments and treaties his relations were exclusively with the Senate, and not with one of its committees.

It is clear that President Washington entertained no such theoretical or practical objections; there are repeated instances of his conferring with committees of the Senate, for the consideration of executive business. While a President may properly decline to recognize any right of the Senate to summon him to the Senate Chamber or to meet with one of its committees, it does not follow that the President and a Senate committee cannot come together in an informal conference for which he has opened the way, without impairing the dignity and prestige of the Senate. The suggestion that in such a personal conference a body of the traditions of the Senate's Committee on Foreign Relations would be so overawed by the President as to lose its independence of judgment is to the highest degree preposterous. Witness, the White House conference over the League of Nations! It should be no less preposterous to assume that in such personal conference with the President, who knows all the intricacies of the negotiation, open-minded Senators might not secure highly valuable light upon the treaty problem awaiting their decision.

Although the Senate's concurrence has often been difficult to obtain and in many cases has led to the delay or failure of treaties, those which receive its consent carry with them the nation's pledge. Senator Lodge proudly asserted:

In the observance of treaties during the last one hundred and twenty-five years there is not a nation in Europe which has been so exact as the United States, nor one which has a record so free from examples of the abrogation of treaties at the pleasure of one of the signers alone.

Whatever satisfaction may be found in the record of the United States' fidelity in the observance of treaties, nevertheless the controversies between Senate and President, the delays and the uncertainties which inevitably in recent years have developed over the ratification of nearly every treaty with a major power and especially over multilateral agreements for the purpose of assuring peace—these are giving rise to serious misunderstandings and distrust.

America [wrote Ray Stannard Baker] has never yet devised a sound or efficient technique of diplomacy. . . . Nearly every important treaty the country has been called upon to make has become a bone of contention between the Executive and the Senate. It is certain that in years to come if we are to go forward in the new paths and stand for a clear-cut world policy, we must devise some method of speaking to the world promptly and with an undivided voice. Our present system leads to utter weakness, muddle and delay; it forces both sides to play politics, and instead of meeting the issue squarely, to indulge in a vast controversy over the prerogatives of two co-ordinate branches of the Government. The deadlock between the Executive and the Senate every time we face a really critical foreign problem is intolerable. It not only disgraces us before the nations, but in some future world crisis may ruin us.

ROLAND N. STROMBERG (1916–   ), who
teaches history at Southern Illinois University,
approaches the League fight from the perspective of
one who is chiefly interested in modern European
intellectual history and in theories and concepts
of foreign policy. In his analysis of the debate over
collective security, he finds that the Republican
opposition was generally sincere, commendable, and
internationalist rather than isolationist. In
viewing Elihu Root as the "key Republican figure"
whose "advice was constantly sought by Lodge
and other prominent Republicans," Stromberg
obviously attaches more importance to what was said
(privately as well as publicly) than to how the
senators voted. Is one a more reliable yardstick than
the other for measuring causes of opposition?*

The Riddle of Article 10

Article 10 was the stumbling block
that prevented American attachment to
the League. The ensuing long and bitter
debate over its meaning was often obscure, yet none the less real. Men *felt*
that a vital issue was involved. Wilson
stated many times that Article 10 was
"the very backbone of the Covenant."
It may be noted that none of his advisers
at Paris (House, Lansing, Tasker Bliss)
had liked it; they feared it would gravely
jeopardize the Treaty before the Senate
while not really adding very much to
the Covenant. Yet the President had
seen the light on this, and his Presbyte-
rian conscience was enlisted. General
Bliss told Thomas Lamont that Wilson
had told his associates the League was
his affair and they were not to butt in.

To say that he was wrong would be ar-
rogant indeed. But it must be recognized
—too often, partisan history has not
done so—that the ambiguity of Article
10 permitted its foes to stand forth
against it with equal sincerity and justification. They did not want the United
States to be in the position of acting dis-
honorably by deciding against going to
war in some unforeseeable future cir-
cumstance. They were understandably
discontent with Wilson's obscure distinction between a legal and a moral obligation. The whole question was about as
confused as it could be. . . .

Article 10, as a flat guarantee of existing frontiers, appeared to freeze the
status quo, and was thus subject to familiar objections. This, Elihu Root re-

---

* From Roland N. Stromberg, *Collective Security and American Foreign Policy, From the League of Nations to NATO* (New York: Frederick A. Praeger, Inc., 1963), pp. 28, 30, 32–39.

marked in his influential criticisms of the Covenant, "would necessarily be futile"; he thought it should be limited to a five-year period, and he later favored its complete elimination. The French and other nations who most ardently wished to defend the new territorial changes were its warmest supporters. This was all well and good, but if Article 10 meant that the League was a kind of alliance of the victors, providing them with security against an enemy they wished to keep in fetters, then it was perhaps inconsistent with the League idea. So, at least, held a large number of the sincerest advocates of internationalism. Moreover, the postwar period produced immediate signs of how uncertain and, as many thought, unjust the new order was. Revolts in Korea, Ireland, Persia, India, and Egypt—to mention just a few of the disturbed places— were in the name of "self-determination" and were not related to the defeated and still hated German enemy. Under these circumstances, to sign up unreservedly for the *status quo* meant, it was widely feared, underwriting colonialism and imperialism. . . .

The other major question was whether the obligations of members to take action against violators of the Covenant, under Article 10 or any other article, were at all binding. In regard to military action, the language was cautious. The Council could "advise," "recommend," "propose" action to the separate member states; it had no will (or military power) of its own. Still, Article 10 indicated an "obligation," and Article 16 made economic sanctions and the severing of diplomatic relations (likely steps toward war) obligatory under certain circumstances. The matter was left in much obscurity and not by accident. Some of the members—those who most

needed protection—wanted these obligations to be binding, while others—those who would have to provide the protection—wanted freedom of action. The risks and the duties were all too clearly not equal under collective security. In the 1920's, Geneva was to become the scene of a struggle between the "potential warrantors" and the "potential warrantees." For the time being, there was much genuine uncertainty. As Root wrote in June in regard to Article 10, "I have seen no defense of it except upon the grounds that the section does not mean what it says." The letters he received from Henry White at Paris were confusing: They indicated, on the one hand, that the League had no coercive power and there was hence no cause for alarm, but, on the other hand that the League was a substitute for war with power to prevent it—much more than "a debating society." This was the way Wilson presented it, too. He did not succeed in making it clear.

This uncertainty provided a double-edged sword of attack on the Covenant. Some feared the possibly unlimited obligations of Article 10. Entanglement in all the broils of a disturbed Europe, underwriting of the British and Japanese empires, American troops summoned abroad at the will of a foreign body—or else the repudiation of a solemn obligation—these were the horrors conjured up by Senator Borah and other eloquent nationalists. At the same time, there were some who feared that the tortuously worded Article 10 was too weak for a firm security system; they would have been more willing to accept a clear-cut military alliance directed against Germany. This was true of the leading Republicans. Theodore Roosevelt, in an editorial written on January 5, 1919, the night before he died, indicated his preference for a League that was frankly a victor's alliance, while Lodge and Root, the masterminds of Republican policy, were sympathetic toward the guarantee treaty, at least for a limited period of time. So also were the *New York Tribune* and Senator P. C. Knox, ex-Secretary of State. Root observed, "If it is necessary for the security of Western Europe that we go to the support of, say, France if attacked, let us agree to do that particular thing plainly. . . . I am in favor of that. But let us not wrap up such a promise in a vague universal obligation."

It seems time to lay to rest the legend of Republican "isolationism" in 1919. Few Americans were more "internationalist" by long habit than Roosevelt, Root, and Lodge, who were more than willing to assume specific international obligations. What they objected to were the confusions of Wilsonian policy. Others too were confused, as newspaper comment abundantly indicates. They had some excuse for it.

No doubt many were in the unhappy situation of a constituent who wrote plaintively to Senator Key Pittman, "My wife and I argued about the League of Nations until our feelings were badly strained and we found it necessary to make up." So began the long fight for the Treaty, with all its pathos and bathos. "The biggest political issue since the days of slavery," the *New York Sun* of March 17, 1919, called it. The pro-League forces, convinced that the very future of the globe was at stake, did not disagree with this estimate by an anti-League organ. The discussion started before the beginning of the Paris Conference, which convened in January, 1919, and continued as the completed Versailles Treaty *cum* League of Nations

Covenant was brought back to the Senate on July 10. Hearings were held from July 31 to September 12, the first big Senate vote came on November 19, and the final vote, after long efforts to arrange a compromise behind the scenes, was on March 19, 1920. Then came the 1920 election, in which the League was a major issue.

Much of the vast body of writings on this affair has been in terms of politics and personalities—the issues, strangely, have been relatively ignored. Everyone is familiar with the personal idiosyncrasies of President Wilson and Senators Lodge and Borah. It used to be fairly orthodox historical doctrine that the Republicans, using the lowest of tricks, killed the League to secure a partisan political advantage. There can be no quarrel with the view that Lodge and Wilson were both stubborn and opinionated men: One of the wisest of living Americans remarked then that the tragedy of the League was that it rested in the hands of the two most obstinate men in American public life, and most historians have agreed. If Lodge was formerly the chief villain, Wilson has tended to assume that role lately; there is generous room for both claims. An almost incredible record of mismanagement of the Senate behind him, the stiff-necked President refused all compromise to the last and, in so doing, lost the respect of much of his own party in the end. It is also true that *both* parties, not unnaturally, sought political advantage from the issue. Perhaps the two-thirds rule was the real villain. Or perhaps it was that feature of the Constitution which condemned a Democratic President to confront a Republican Congress —with a Presidential election coming up.

There is also the question of how far

Wilson was thrown off his course by his illness. It seems clear that this has been exaggerated at times. It is amazing how many superficial accounts speak of him as a "dying man," or even have him practically in the grave by 1920. Actually, Wilson lived until 1924 and was capable of clear thought until the end; at least, he wrote coherent magazine articles in 1923. He quarreled with most of his old friends, but this was not an altogether new trait. Though undeniably subjected by physician and wife to a sickroom quarantine in the critical months of 1919–20 that kept away such moderating influences as that of Colonel House, Wilson remained quite rational and in touch with the debate, and his course may not have been much affected by his illness. And it must be considered similarly questionable that had his speaking tour not been interrupted by the illness, Wilson would have carried the League to victory. More plausible is the opinion that his inability to present the League in an adequate light helped bring on his breakdown.

It is not in our province to dispose of such questions as these. We may suggest, however, that the League itself, and especially the idea of collective security, had something to do with the Senate's rejection of it. It was against the background of great issues that Lodge, Borah, and Wilson strutted their proud parts; it is singular that so much of the history of this episode does not even analyze the issues, having spent its time psychoanalyzing the men. A sounder interpretation of the League controversy would be one that portrayed men of reasonably good will struggling to decipher the meaning of the League system and to reconcile it with legitimate national interest—and in the end finding themselves baffled.

A huge majority of the Senators (seventy-nine out of ninety-six) were in favor of approving the Treaty and entering the League with some sort of reasonable "reservations." President Wilson himself acceded, though reluctantly and somewhat belatedly, to six "interpretive" resolutions.[1] Senator Lodge and the Republicans came up with fourteen, of which the great majority were calculated to annoy rather than to amend drastically. It was agreed by all (after some preliminary confusion) that "reservations" were conceivably not amendments—that is, they might require no change in the Covenant itself but would only express the American interpretation. Most Democrats held, however, that the Lodge reservations were really amendments in the sense that they actually modified the Treaty.[2] Gravely weak-

---

[1] Prior to his speaking tour in September, Wilson gave his consent privately to four resolutions of interpretation for future use, but later withdrew it. After the Senate defeat of November 19 and during the subsequent efforts to work out a compromise, Senator Hitchcock, the Democratic floor leader, got full party support, including Wilson's, for six "interpretive" resolutions, but the President showed a certain coolness toward them and remained publicly silent. During this period, as Stephen Bonsal has related, Wilson rejected a peace offer tendered by Senator Lodge through Bonsal and Colonel House. He had now broken with his old friend House. Mrs. Wilson, in her memoirs, indicates that the Wilsons thought it treason for House even to confer with the "archenemy" Lodge.

[2] The more significant of the Lodge reservations other than the vital one on Article 10 dealt with (a) making the exclusion of the Monroe Doctrine from the jurisdiction of the League more specific (it was already excluded, but the language was not blunt enough to suit the Republicans); (b) specifically, rather than by implication, excluding all domestic questions from the League's jurisdiction; and (c) making the right of withdrawal from the League clearer than it was. The substantive issue was vital in none of these, there being only a question of language; but here, as on the more important matter of Article 10, the Wilsonian philosophy was to avoid saying bluntly what was implied

ening this position were indications from both France and Great Britain that they were willing to look upon the Lodge reservations as interpretations not requiring any further action by the other signatories. But Wilson refused to be moved by this, and even refused to see Lord Grey when he made a trip to this country early in 1920.

After the vote of November 19, there seemed an excellent chance for compromise. Letters in the papers of prominent men indicate strong pressure from leading citizens in favor of a compromise, and there were moments when Borah despaired of defeating the League. Among various polls conducted, a typical one taken in the colleges and universities showed 39 per cent favoring compromise, 30 per cent for unconditional ratification, 17 per cent for ratification with the Lodge reservations, and 14 per cent for outright rejection. "The fairly universal opinion is," John H. Finley wrote to Senator Pittman on December 31, "that the differences are too small to warrant failure to come to an agreement, that with two or three exceptions the proposed reservations are justified in substance, and it only needs that they be phrased less raspingly." There were numerous other letters to the same effect. Most journalistic comment expected a compromise, though some was skeptical.

Efforts to bridge the gap broke down

---

while the Republicans acted in terms of Lodge's statement that "if it goes without saying there can be no harm in saying it." (Bonsal, *Unfinished Business*, p. 275.) Among the other reservations, the objection to giving each of the British Dominions a separate vote was political pettiness; the objection to Japan's position in Shantung, popular but not very directly related to the League Covenant. (The Covenant, of course, was a part of the general peace settlement, being incorporated in the Treaty of Versailles—a controversial decision.)

on the issue of Article 10. Much importance has been attached (not least by Senator Borah himself) to the dramatic threat of Borah, Hiram Johnson, and several other "irreconcilables" to bolt the Republican Party if Lodge yielded on this issue, but it seems unlikely that this was decisive. Efforts continued to be made to find a formula that would reconcile Wilson's insistence on the "obligation" with the firm belief of others that there must not be any obligation. This word became the great stumbling block. The reality underlying it was a stubborn ambiguity at the heart of "collective security" itself.

Wilson became willing to support an interpretative reservation to the effect that the United States was free to reject any advice offered by the League Council concerning violations of Article 10. Everyone agreed that Congress had to make up its mind whether or not the United States wished to use any military force at the time of the request to do so and not before. Certainly, Wilson never imagined that there would be any automatic obligation to send troops if we joined the League, and he was willing to say so. (He *had* said so many times at Paris.) But he insisted that there was an obligation of some sort as Article 10 plainly read, whereas the opposition wished to repudiate the obligation. Both positions were reasonable, in a way. Wilson believed that to say, with Lodge, that the United States assumed no obligation, constituted a plain alteration of the language of the Covenant and thus was an amendment to which other states would have to agree, and that the psychological effect of denying any obligation would be disastrous to the League system. Even when reaction abroad partly demolished the first point, the second evidently remained for him sufficiently forceful to prevent any compromise. The fact is that the issue, on the question of "obligation," was essentially uncompromisable. Effort after effort was made to find a linguistic formula that would save the day, but without success. Either an obligation existed or it did not; it is difficult to conceive of a semi-obligation. Like sovereignty—or chastity—it would seem to be all of a piece, incapable of being just partly there.

The Republicans insisted, and continued to insist, that if the United States admitted an obligation that she subsequently refused to honor, she put herself in a false and potentially humiliating position. The point was strong enough to impress not merely Senator Lodge, but all the pro-League Republicans who later signed the Statement of the Thirty-one: Herbert Hoover, Elihu Root, Henry L. Stimson, Taft,[3] Lowell, Butler, *et al.* These were men whose internationalism predated Wilson's and whose experience exceeded his in many cases; they wanted a League as much as Wilson. Their point was basically that if an obligation was admitted, then any refusal by Congress at some future date to respond to a war call from the League would be "a breach of the solemnly pledged faith of the United States." It would also be, conceivably, a cruel blow to international cooperation itself. *Ergo,* it must be made clear that there was no obligation.

In effect, Wilson and the Democrats wanted to accept an obligation that we might thereafter refuse, while Lodge and the Republicans wanted to refuse an obligation we might thereafter accept. Underlying this wordplay, which may seem unreal, were the very real ambiguities

of the League itself. What men wanted to do was both to accept and to qualify an international obligation. The Wilsonians were led into the desert because, when it came down to it, they had seen how impossible it was to give the League any real power. They tried to repair the damage by insisting on the word "obligation," chiefly for its psychological effect. They knew and said that Congress alone could commit the nation to war, and they must have known that so grave a decision would never be taken merely because of any words in a treaty. But they strove valiantly by effort of will to make collective security meaningful. As for the Republicans, they came to see, ever more clearly, that the League would not be any worker of miracles; it would be, almost inevitably, hardly more than the sum of the separate states. Accused of having little faith, they replied that their foes had little sense if they could not see this. "It may be noble thinking, but it is not true thinking," Robert Lansing commented laconically on the collective-security theory. Lansing elsewhere analyzed Wilson's thinking as based on "intuition rather than reason." It was a shrewd diagnosis. The clash was between types of minds, and it is fair to say that the faith of the Wilsonians was matched by their fuzziness when it came to concrete cases.

It has happened too often in writing the history of this episode that justice has not been done to the Republican side. Let Root again serve; he was the key Republican figure, and his advice was constantly sought by Lodge and other prominent Republicans throughout the Senate battle. The following analysis is based on a study of his letters and papers in the Library of Congress:

He thought the League had fallen between two stools, being both too ambi-

---

[3] Taft did not sign the Statement but said he would have had he been reached in time.

tious and too weak, through confusing the limited purposes of postwar reconstruction with the larger ones of permanent peace. For the latter, Root held to "the judicial settlement of international disputes and the development of international law"—which, he complained, had been neglected at Paris. The short term he thought required something like an Article 10, which at first he favored keeping with a five-year time limit. His views in that connection have already been mentioned. He came to consider Article 10 an "incredible mistake" because it meant either nothing or the impossible, requiring the United States to fight to defend any member of the League at any time, "no matter what our people at the time think about the right and wrong of the controversy." He found Wilson's distinction between a legal and a moral obligation "demoralizing and destructive" because he believed it argued, in effect, that a treaty is meaningless. We were to agree to an "obligation," but we might or might not honor it. Wilson's position seemed to him "inconsistent and irreconcilable."

Root had been irritated by what he regarded as Wilson's dictatorial methods, and by the President's efforts to brand anyone who wanted a reservation as an enemy of the entire scheme and *ergo* of the human race. Root thought Wilson was saying that "Anyone who does not swallow the agreement whole is opposed to peace," and he bitterly resented it. There were other incidents contributing to a personal estrangement. Yet, it seems unlikely that the equable Root was dominated by personal animus, and even more unlikely that partisan political motives played more than a minor part in his case (he was now old, retired from public life, a famous and respected "elder statesman"). Patient realist that

he was, Root, the classical conservative, felt that something should and could be salvaged. To him, the reasonable solution was clear: A few reservations were essential, their substance should be obvious, and the Allies ought to be apprised of them. He did not think there was much danger that the Allies would object to them—and herein he proved to be right. He did not favor flamboyant statements; for example, in regard to Shantung, against which there had been strong feeling in the Senate (because of the seemingly cynical awarding of Chinese territory to Japan as war booty), he advised telling the Allies "quietly" that we did not approve of the settlement and could not be a party to arrangements made prior to our entrance into the war (a prior secret treaty was the case here). Most essential, however, was a general reservation in regard to the "obligation" under Article 10.

Root did not agree with those radical foes of the Treaty who wished to kill it altogether; he did not think membership in the League unconstitutional. On the other hand, it would appear that he felt little need for a League of Nations as such: A treaty of alliance for certain specific and temporary purposes on the one hand and, on the other, an international judicial tribunal were his goals. A political League was less valuable than a world court, and an ambiguous Article 10 less valuable than a straight-out alliance with France. To him, the Covenant confused the two realms of necessary present darkness and eventual light by mingling them. Moreover, the value attached to a continuation of the military alliance of World War I undeniably faded in 1920 and 1921, and this was a strong factor in Wilson's defeat. As the emotions of the war wore off, Germany in 1920 seemed less likely to be a menace to Europe as a military power than as a vacuum susceptible to Communism or decay. In his speech to the Republican Convention in New York on February 19, 1920, Root declared that to bind the United States to one side would not serve the cause of peace.

Republican policy in the 1920's was to be consistent in bringing forth the Kellogg Pact and the World Court as saner alternatives to the League. These had been the Root policies from the beginning, and the Root policies came close to being the Republican policies. Among the many senators who applied to him for advice in 1919 were Lodge and Frank B. Kellogg.

In contrast to Stromberg, W. STULL HOLT (1896–) emphasizes the insincere and "unworthy causes of opposition" to the League. His study of the Senate votes on the reservations and the final resolutions of ratification (technically, resolutions of approval, not ratification) convinced him that party politics, not the Constitution or ideology, essentially dictated the outcome of the fight. Some writers have found his evidence based upon voting records less persuasive for the fourth and final vote in March 1920 than for the first three votes in November 1919. Holt's scholarly interests include historiography and the urban movement in addition to American foreign policy. Most of his academic life has been spent at the University of Washington, although he has also been on the staff of the Brookings Institution and in 1963–1964 was editor of the *American Historical Review*.*

Playing Politics with the League

When the voting began in October, no steps had been taken by the Democrats to reach an understanding with the Republicans wanting mild reservations and the latter were drifting toward a politically natural alliance with their fellow Republicans on terms more hostile to the treaty than those they would have preferred. In the votes on the amendments proposed both by the Committee on Foreign Relations and by individual senators the mild reservationists joined with the almost solid Democratic membership and all the amendments were lost. On November 7, the voting began on the reservations and then the mild reservationists united with the balance of the Republicans. Belated efforts by the Democrats to detach the mild reservationists by offering to accept in-

terpretative reservations failed completely. Equally futile were the frantic last minute appeals to the mild reservationists not to assist the Republicans who had always wanted to kill the treaty by voting for reservations they had earlier condemned as being equivalent to rejection. The Republican ranks held firmly together. The final position of the mild reservationists was described by one of them in these terms. When the administration forces declined to listen to any efforts at agreement the "middle ground Senators found themselves obliged to commit themselves to the Lodge program after concessions were made by the radicals, and they now are unable to break away."

As reservation after reservation was added to the treaty by the unbroken Re-

---

* From W. Stull Holt, *Treaties Defeated by the Senate* (Baltimore: Johns Hopkins Press, 1933), pp. 292–307. Some footnotes omitted.

Table 1   Votes on the Versailles Treaty by Parties

		November, 1919		March, 1920	
		Yea	Nay	Yea	Nay
Preamble	Democrats	3	39		
	Republicans	45	1		
Reservation No. 1 (Withdrawal)	Democrats	5	35	10	20
	Republicans	45	0	35	0
Reservation No. 2 (Article 10)	Democrats	4	33	14	26
	Republicans	42	0	42	0
Reservation No. 3 (Mandates)	Democrats	9	31	30	4
	Republicans	41	0	38	0
Reservation No. 4 (Domestic questions)	Democrats	10	36	14	25
	Republicans	49	0	42	0
Reservation No. 5 (Monroe Doctrine)	Democrats	9	34	17	22
	Republicans	46	0	41	0
Reservation No. 6 (Shantung)	Democrats	5	40	10	21
	Republicans	48	1	38	0
Reservation No. 7 (Appointment of representatives)	Democrats	5	40	17	14
	Republicans	48	0	38	0
Reservation No. 8 (Reparations commission)	Democrats	5	40	6	22
	Republicans	49	0	35	0
Reservation No. 9 (Expenses of League)	Democrats	7	39	8	25
	Republicans	49	0	38	0
Reservation No. 10 (Armaments)	Democrats	7	39	9	26
	Republicans	49	0	40	0
Reservation No. 11 (Covenant-breaking states)	Democrats	5	41	5	28
	Republicans	48	0	39	0
Reservation No. 12 (Illegal acts)	Democrats	4	41	8	26
	Republicans	48	0	37	1
Reservation No. 13 (International labor)	Democrats	8	34	6	27
	Republicans	46	1	38	0
Reservation No. 14 (Dominion votes)	Democrats	8	37	17	20
	Republicans	47	1	40	0
Reservation No. 15 (Irish self-determination)	Democrats			21	16
	Republicans			17	20
Ratification With Reservations	Democrats	4	42	21	23
	Republicans	35	13	28	12
Ratification Without Reservations	Democrats	37	7		
	Republicans	1	46		

publican majority, some friends of the league in alarm pled with the Democrats to accept what could be gotten rather than lose everything. Senator McCumber made such a plea immediately before the vote was taken. Other sincere advocates of the league who were not members of the Senate urged the same course. On the day of the final vote a mild reser-vationist read into the *Record* a statement by the executive committee of the League to Enforce Peace condemning some of the reservations, yet advising their acceptance since the league could still accomplish its purpose. These pleas, too, fell on deaf ears. At a conference of Democratic senators held before the final vote Senator Hitchcock read a letter from the White House in which the President called upon the friends and supporters of the treaty to vote against the Lodge resolution of ratification because the reservations in it nullified the treaty.

Consequently when the Senate voted on the treaty it failed to receive a two-thirds vote both with and without reservations. With the fourteen reservations it was rejected by a vote of 39 to 55.[1] Without the reservations it was rejected by a vote of 38 to 53. An analysis of the final votes and the decisive vote on each reservation (Table 1) reveals the controlling influence of party politics. The reservations were added by practically solid Republican votes. Three times, on the preamble and on reservations 6 and 14, Senator McCumber left his party, as did Senator Sherman on reservation 13. With those rare exceptions the Republicans were unanimous on the reservations every one of which needed only the Republican votes it received to be adopted. The Democrats were practically, although not absolutely, as united as the Republicans on the reservations. There was a handful of Democrats who voted for all the reservations and on the less important reservations several others deserted the party ranks. On the final votes the Democrats voted 42 to 4 against ratification with the reservations, and 37 to 7 in favor of ratification without reservations. The Republicans preserved their unity in voting against ratification without reservations, the vote being 46 to 1. Only McCumber left the party ranks. But on the vote for ratification with the reservations a decided break occurred. Thirteen Republicans, all irreconcilables, refused to go with the party major-

ity. Nevertheless, the Republicans cast more than two-thirds of their votes for the treaty with reservations, the numbers being 35 for and 13 against. The refusal of the thirteen irreconcilable Republicans to remain with their party did not affect the result because the nearly solid Democratic vote would have prevented the ratification of the treaty with reservations.

When the same votes are analyzed by groups rather than by party affiliation, the importance of the irreconcilables in deciding the issue becomes more apparent. (Table 2). The irreconcilables occupied a strong position because of the peculiar rule of the Senate which, since 1868, permitted amendments to be inserted or reservations added by an ordinary majority although a two-thirds majority was necessary on the final vote of ratification. There were 39 Democrats who voted against the treaty with reservations. There were 39 senators, 35 Republicans and 4 Democrats, who wanted the treaty with reservations. Since the reservationists did not constitute a majority no reservations could have been added without the votes of the 17 irreconcilables.[2] As a matter of fact the

[1] There was one vacancy in the Senate when the vote was taken. Senator Fall was absent but was recorded as being opposed to the treaty either with or without reservations.

[2] There has been much confusion and inaccuracy regarding the number of irreconcilables, or senators against the treaty either with or without reservations. This is due in part to the fact that one was absent on the final vote and in part to the fact that the membership of the group changed between the vote in November and the vote in March. In November there were 14 Republicans in the group: Borah, Brandegee, Fernald, France, Gronna, Johnson, Knox, La Follette, McCormick, Moses, Norris, Poindexter, Sherman and Fall. Fall was absent on the final vote but had voted with the irreconcilables on reservations and was paired against the treaty without reservations. His opposition to the treaty in any form was announced and he must properly be included with the irreconcilables. There were 3 Democratic irreconcilables in November, Reed, Thomas and Trammel. The case of the last name was peculiar. He several times stated publicly he was for the treaty. New York *Times*,

Table 2   Votes on the Versailles Treaty by Groups

		November, 1919		March, 1920	
		Yea	Nay	Yea	Nay
Preamble	Advocates	0	36		
	Reservationists	33	2		
	Irreconcilables	15	2		
Reservation No. 1	Advocates	1	33	6	19
(Withdrawn)	Reservationists	34	0	28	0
	Irreconcilables	15	2	12	1
Reservation No. 2	Advocates	0	31	9	25
(Article 10)	Reservationists	33	0	33	1
	Irreconcilables	13	2	14	0
Reservation No. 3	Advocates	3	30	24	4
(Mandates)	Reservationists	34	0	33	0
	Irreconcilables	15	1	11	0
Reservation No. 4	Advocates	3	36	8	25
(Domestic questions)	Reservationists	39	0	34	0
	Irreconcilables	17	0	14	0
Reservation No. 5	Advocates	3	33	11	22
(Monroe Doctrine)	Reservationists	38	1	34	0
	Irreconcilables	14	0	13	0
Reservation No. 6	Advocates	0	38	5	20
(Shantung)	Reservationists	37	2	30	1
	Irreconcilables	16	1	13	0
Reservation No. 7	Advocates	0	38	11	14
(Appointment of representatives)	Reservationists	39	0	31	0
	Irreconcilables	14	2	13	0
Reservation No. 8	Advocates	0	38	2	20
(Reparations commission)	Reservationists	39	0	29	1
	Irreconcilables	15	2	10	1

Democrats did not always muster their full strength against the reservations, but their leaders would have gotten out the votes had not the affirmative votes of the irreconcilables removed any doubts as to the outcome. So the irreconcilables first joined one group in putting reservations into the resolution of ratification and then voted against the resolution with the third group whose opposition was caused by those reservations.

The rejection of the treaty caused great amazement and immediately a

widespread demand arose for renewed efforts to effect a compromise. It seemed absurd that the national policy adopted should be the one advocated by only 17 senators. Common sense revolted at seeing the votes of 78 senators to enter the league nullified because they could not agree among themselves on the terms of entry. Many Republican newspapers and Republican leaders outside the Senate joined with the Democrats in refusing to accept the decision reached by such means. Spurred on by this pressure the mild reservationists began to seek a basis for common action with the Democrats. After a number had agreed upon tentative terms the leaders of the two parties were added to the group which became known as the "Bi-partisan Conference." Notwithstanding the presence of Lodge

Sept. 28, 1919; *Congressional Record*, Nov. 18, 1919, p. 8738. Nevertheless he voted against it in both forms. In March, however, he voted for it with reservations. He was the only one who left the irreconcilable group in March while Shields, a Democrat, and Penrose, a Republican, who had both voted for the treaty with reservations went against it in March, making 18 irreconcilables on the second test.

Table 2   Votes on the Versailles Treaty by Groups (cont.)

		November, 1919		March, 1920	
		Yea	Nay	Yea	Nay
Reservation No. 9	Advocates	1	38	3	24
(Expenses of League)	Reservationists	39	0	29	1
	Irreconcilables	16	1	14	0
Reservation No. 10	Advocates	1	38	5	25
(Armaments)	Reservationists	39	0	31	1
	Irreconcilables	16	1	13	0
Reservation No. 11	Advocates	0	39	2	27
(Covenant-breaking states)	Reservationists	38	0	30	1
	Irreconcilables	15	2	12	0
Reservation No. 12	Advocates	0	38	5	26
(Illegal acts)	Reservationists	37	1	28	1
	Irreconcilables	15	2	12	0
Reservation No. 13	Advocates	2	33	2	26
(International labor)	Reservationists	38	0	29	1
	Irreconcilables	14	2	13	0
Reservation No. 14	Advocates	2	36	11	20
(Dominion votes)	Reservationists	38	1	33	0
	Irreconcilables	15	1	13	0
Reservation No. 15	Advocates			17	13
(Irish self-determination)	Reservationists			11	22
	Irreconcilables			10	1
Ratification With Reservations	Advocates	0	39	17	20
	Reservationists	39	0	32	0
	Irreconcilables	0	16	0	15
Ratification Without Reservations	Advocates	37	0		
	Reservationists	1	37		
	Irreconcilables	0	16		

such progress was made in the discussions, which were kept secret, that newspapers of all persuasions stated that the deadlock was nearly broken and the prospects for passing the treaty were bright. This situation called forth storms of protest from the irreconcilables as well as threats of leaving the party. There is a dramatic story that on January 23, 1920, they called Lodge from what was to be the crucial meeting of the Bi-partisan Conference and harangued him for three hours in Senator Johnson's office during which time the conference got tired of waiting and adjourned. However, in view of the record, it is doubtful that Lodge would have accepted any significant reductions in his reservations so long as the mild reservationists did not threaten to leave the party on that issue. The danger of a secession by them proved to be easily averted. Lodge kept them with him even when the Democrats offered to accept the Taft reservation to Article 10, "the heart of the covenant,"—a reservation which expressly disavowed any obligation and which, therefore, conceded all that the Republicans wanted, according to Lodge's statement of two days earlier.

In spite of the failure of the Bi-partisan Conference to reach an agreement the treaty again came before the Senate. On February 9 the Senate reconsidered its vote of November 19 and sent the treaty back to committee, on the next day it was reported to the Senate from committee, and on February 16 the debate was resumed. This second vote, taken in deference to public opinion, constituted a test of the loyalty of the Democrats to Wilson and of their determination to adhere to their former course. Everyone realized that the Republican senators would preserve their unity in passing the Lodge reservations without essential changes. Everyone knew how the irreconcilables would then vote on the resolution of ratification. The only question open was whether enough Democrats would consider there was no other alternative and would prefer the Lodge reservations to a complete rejection. Again many undoubtedly sincere advocates of the league pled with the Democrats to take what was possible. But again Wilson wrote a letter from his sick-bed in the White House urging his Democratic followers to stand firm against nullifying reservations. The Lodge reservation to Article 10, he wrote, "cuts at the very heart and life of the covenant itself." After explaining the reasons for this statement, he gave his conclusion that "either we should enter the league fearlessly, accepting the responsibility and not fearing the role of leadership which we now enjoy, . . . or we should retire as gracefully as possible from the great concert of powers by which the world was saved." Wilson still hoped that public opinion would compel the ratification of the treaty with no more than interpretative reservations and his faith in the people made him willing to wait for the approaching national election.

The final vote in the Senate took place on March 19, 1920. Before then the fourteen Lodge reservations had again been made a part of the resolution of ratification with a few immaterial verbal changes, and to them was added a new reservation expressing sympathy with the "aspirations of the Irish people for a government of their own choice." With these fifteen reservations the resolution of ratification received a majority

of the votes cast but not the requisite two-thirds majority, 49 votes being in favor of it and 35 being opposed.[3]

The analysis of the voting during this second struggle over the treaty discloses some significant similarities and contrasts with the voting in November. As before, the Republican senators cast a practically solid party vote for the Lodge reservations. The only exception was the vote of Senator Nelson against the twelfth reservation. In contrast with this Republican unity the Democrats split decidedly and many more of them than on the former occasion voted for the Lodge reservations. The fifteenth reservation concerning Irish independence was a Democratic contribution. It was introduced by a Democrat and it alone of the reservations was put in by Democratic votes since more than half of the Republicans who voted opposed it. There were Democrats who, like Lodge, appreciated the importance of the Irish vote to their party. On the final vote of ratification the Republican ranks broke as they had in November. Twenty-eight of the Republican senators, or more than two-thirds of the number voting, favored the ratification of the treaty with the reservations. Twelve Republicans again deserted their party and voted against ratification with reservations. The Democrats voting divided almost equally, 21 for ratification and 23 against.

Of the 21 Democrats voting for the treaty, 4 were reservationists who had refused to vote for the treaty without reservations in November. The other 17, and the 2 Democrats paired in favor of the treaty refused for the first time to

---

[3] Eight senators were paired in favor of the treaty against four who would have voted in the negative had they not been paired. Six of the eight were Republicans, and three of the four recorded in the negative were Republicans. Hence of the total membership of the Senate 57 were recorded in favor of the resolution of ratification and 39 against it.

support the policy of their party leaders. They too had wanted the treaty without any reservations, but preferred to take what was offered rather than to risk losing all. Of the 23 Democrats who opposed the treaty, 3 were irreconcilables and 20 were senators who had voted for the treaty without reservations in November and against it with the Lodge reservations. These 20, and the one Democrat paired in the negative, followed Wilson's advice and leadership. All of them were from Southern states except Hitchcock of Nebraska and Johnson of South Dakota. Had Wilson not used his influence on the Democrats the resolution of ratification would certainly have passed, since a two-thirds majority would have been obtained if only seven of this loyal band of 21 had transferred their votes.

Wilson's success in commanding the support of some of the Democratic senators shared responsibility for the rejection of the treaty with Lodge's failure as a leader. If Lodge had been able to hold all the Republican senators to the program of his party, the treaty would have received the approval of the Senate by an ample margin. But the irreconcilable Republicans, increased to the number of 15 by the addition of Penrose, repeated their desertion of November. After voting solidly with their party in favor of the reservations that made 21 Democrats oppose the treaty, they left their fellow-Republicans and joined the 21 Democrats in opposition. Twelve of them voted in the negative on the resolution of ratification, the other three being paired on the same side. Thus the policy of the Republican party was defeated by this break in its ranks. As the party leader Lodge had failed. As a true irreconcilable himself, he could view his management with satisfaction although it meant the conquest of the majority he led by the minority of his party.

Notwithstanding the deceptive division of both parties on the final vote, politics had killed another treaty—the most distinguished on its long list of victims. There were, however, other considerations that helped determine the action of the Senate. None of these minor factors had as much weight as the senatorial desire to assert the Senate's powers in making treaties. The Senate was the equal partner of the President in making treaties. The Senate must protect its powers from an autocratic President by insisting upon altering the treaty he had signed. That refrain was constantly present throughout the entire controversy, accentuating and supplementing the dominant theme of politics. It was on appeals to the Senate's jealousy of its powers that the irreconcilables chiefly depended in their early efforts to rally the Republican majority to an attack on Wilson's program. Scarcely a speech was made by the opposition in which some variation of this idea was not included.

To have the Senate alter or reject a treaty merely as a means of asserting its powers against the President was nothing new. As Viscount Grey explained to a bewildered British public, "The American Constitution not only makes possible, but under certain conditions renders inevitable, a conflict between the Executive and the Legislature." In 1919 conditions were such that the conflict was not only inevitable but was certain to be ruthless. The war had made Wilson a dictator and had reduced Congress to negligible proportions both in power and in public attention. The crisis had compelled Congress to do what the President wanted or to sanction what he had already done. Once the war was ended the Senate, as the stronger branch of Congress, attempted to restore the balance of power in the government. Consequently the treaty of peace containing the outstanding issue of the period was certain to serve as a battleground, and one where the Senate was in an advantageous position because of the constitutional provision requiring a two-thirds majority. Moreover, the Senate received more public support in its contest than under ordinary circumstances. The dictatorship had irritated many, even of those who had wanted it. They and all who had been forced to suppress their hostility to Wilson's policies now applauded the senators opposing the President with the cry of "no autocracy."

Probably there were few in or out of the Senate who honestly believed it would have been proper for the Senate to execute the plan suggested by Senator Cummins. Before the peace conference opened, that defender of the Senate's prerogatives introduced a resolution into the Senate providing that eight senators should proceed to the conference and acquaint themselves with everything that transpired. The mere suggestion of such a plan for the first time in the history of the United States was significant. The same claim that the Senate should participate in the negotiations was made by others. Senator Lodge . . . demanded that procedure on a number of occasions, notably in his speech of December 21, 1918. With an amazing disregard of both his former statements and precedent he tried to make it appear that the President departed from American tradition by not consulting the Senate during the negotiations. The senators who signed the round-robin expressed the same theory and were attempting to act on it.

Although these efforts to extend the powers of the Senate to the extent of participating in the making of the treaty failed, they did create an atmosphere favorable to the re-making of the treaty when the Senate had its opportunity. The impression spread that the Presi-

dent had invaded the rights of the Senate. Time after time this note was struck. A typical example occurred in a speech by Senator Spencer. "The President," he asserted, "alone pursued his course, without any conference with the country he represented and with special disregard of the Senate, which, by the Constitution of the United States is made his legal adviser, particularly in connection with treaties." The results of this attitude can be seen not only in the insistence of senators on changes merely as a method of vindicating their powers but also in the changes made. A number of the reservations defined the way in which the United States should reach a decision in certain cases and each time the powers of Congress were specifically protected. The most glaring instance of this was in the first reservation which stated that a notice of withdrawal from the league might be given by a concurrent resolution of the Congress of the United States. A concurrent resolution requires a majority of both houses of Congress but not the signature of the President so the latter was not to participate in the making of that important decision. Indeed the hostility of the Senate toward the Executive was so strong and so disastrous for the treaty that two Republican mild reservationists made the statement—astounding in the American Congress—that they favored a parliamentary system in which such friction was impossible. The victory of the Senate over the President ushered in a period during which the Senate dictated foreign policy as it had never done before.

Yet the constitutional struggle of the Senate against the President was subordinated to politics. Only Republicans entered the battle in defense of the Senate's prerogatives. The Democrats, with the exception of the very few who fought Wilson, saw no invasion of the rights of the Senate. This division proved the supremacy of political considerations. A Republican senator gave evidence to the same effect. In speaking of the first reservation McCumber said, "I am satisfied that if we had a Republican President today we would not be insisting that he should be eliminated from any voice in the matter of any future action that we might take in respect to staying in or getting out of this league of nations."

Politics and the contest over the treaty-making power were not the only forces in the Senate operating against the Versailles treaty. A third, although relatively minor, factor was the personal hatred of Wilson which other senators besides Lodge felt. Wilson aroused more hatred than any President since the days of Lincoln and Johnson. Naturally no senator publicly admitted either the sentiment or its influence. Nevertheless it was reflected in many speeches, and other senators believed it swayed some individuals. Senator Walsh of Montana, who did not indulge in intemperate statements, evidently believed it a factor of importance. "I undertake to say," he asserted, "that nine out of ten letters I get in protest against this treaty breathe a spirit of intense hatred of Woodrow Wilson . . . , and I am led to believe that that feeling forms a very large element in the opposition to this treaty; but I am astounded that Senators of the United States should allow considerations of that character to influence their judgment."

Combined with these three unworthy causes of opposition was a fourth which was entirely proper. This was the desire to return to the traditional policy of isolation. Some persons must have believed sincerely in the superior wisdom of that policy and must have reached that conclusion through a judgment on the merits of the two policies and not through political or other irrelevant prejudices. The public which with no discernible exceptions had approved the new policy began to swing back in the other direction. Undoubtedly the recrudescence of isolationism was also felt in the Senate. The extent to which it influenced individual senators cannot be measured. But it can be asserted with as much certainty as is possible in human affairs that a sincere belief based on the merits of the issue was not the dominant cause of the Senate's action. It was the reservations that killed the treaty. And in adopting them the Senate divided on party lines, all the Republicans for them and practically all the Democrats against them. Such a division eliminates all doubts.

The fate of the treaty of Versailles turned the attention of thoughtful people to the treaty-making power of the United States. They saw that the exercise of that power had produced such bitter conflicts between the President and the Senate and had so increased the opportunities for political warfare unconnected with the merits of the question that many treaties had been lost. They knew that the ratification of nearly every important treaty had been endangered by a constitutional system which, instead of permitting a decision solely on the merits of the question, produces impotence and friction. They realized that if no disaster had resulted it was due partly to good fortune and chiefly to the relative unimportance of foreign relations in the history of the United States so that few treaties had contained vital issues. They also realized that, if the United States was to play the part in world affairs demanded by its interests and its strength, a deadlock between the President and the Senate over a treaty involving a really critical foreign problem may end in ruin.

One of the surprisingly few books on the subject of American isolationism is by SELIG ADLER (1909–   ), Samuel P. Capen Professor of American History, State University of New York at Buffalo. According to Adler, the rejection of the League is best understood within the context of the isolationist tradition. Temporarily eclipsed by wartime expressions of utopian internationalism, isolationism burst into the open during the League debates. Comprising so many powerful elements, it was not to be denied. Note that Adler's interpretation differs from Holt's as well as from Stromberg's.*

The Isolationist Impulse

Every thinking person who ponders recent history is tantalized by the question: would the subsequent years have been different if the United States had supported the League of Nations in 1919? Such speculation, however intriguing, provides no satisfactory conclusion, for the simple fact remains that we did not join. Why then, one might continue, did Woodrow Wilson succeed in fashioning a League of Nations at the Versailles Peace Conference only to fail to convince his own country of the necessity for collective security? After one hundred years of relative indifference to foreign affairs, a reaction against our first overseas venture was probably inevitable. Before Wilson had reached a single decision at Paris a stout opposition was brewing. To overcome his opponents, the President had to have support above and beyond his normal Democratic strength. He needed a coalition behind him. Instead of creating this bulwark, the Versailles treaty itself engendered three powerful counter movements. . . .

The defection of the liberals was the first great factor in the combination against Wilson. It provided the conservative-nationalists with the overwhelming argument that the President had been repudiated by his own followers. It destroyed a vocal source that hitherto had argued for a Wilsonian peace and shattered the alliance between the political

* Reprinted from *The Isolationist Impulse, Its Twentieth Century Reaction* by Selig Adler, pp. 54–59, 73–78, 92–117. By permission of Abelard-Schuman Ltd. All rights reserved. Copyright year 1957.

independents and the Democrats which for so long had strengthened the Chief Executive's position.

To understand this defection it is necessary to explore the problems that Wilson met at Versailles, for it was his solutions to these questions that alienated men of liberal persuasion. When the peace conference opened on January 12, 1919, the President found himself at grips with stark reality. He faced David Lloyd George of Great Britain, Georges Clemenceau of France, Vittorio Orlando of Italy, and the Japanese diplomats. These men mirrored nationalist and imperialist aspirations, the wartime punitive spirit, and their people's hunger for reparations. There were also secret treaty promises to be cashed in at the peace table. France and Italy insisted upon boundary adjustments for reasons of national security and ambition. Such demands ran counter to Wilson's formula of self-determination for subject peoples. All of the victorious powers, with the exception of the United States, cast greedy eyes on German and Turkish colonial possessions. Wilson had to compromise or else go home, because his opponents could not yield completely and still remain in office. Their flexibility was limited for they had fanned the hopes of their war-torn constituents by promises of "squeezing Germany till the pips squeaked," of boundary extensions, and of post-war security.

Wilson could not choose to leave. Bolshevism appeared to be spreading westward from a Russia that was capitalizing on fluid boundaries and internal disorder in new states. Wilson saw but one alternative. He would fight tenaciously for as much of his program as he could salvage. His prime objective was an organization to maintain peace. To achieve it he would make concessions

on other stipulations. In the fullness of time, the President reasoned, an effective League would rectify the injustices engendered by the passions of the moment. To guarantee the birth of a living league, Wilson insisted that the Covenant of the League of Nations be incorporated into all the treaties of peace. As these agreements were ratified, nations would automatically become members of the new organization.

Wilson had decided that he would let the end justify the means. In taking this step he put himself in a vulnerable position. Had his original program embraced merely American national interests, such demands could have been compromised without due loss of face. They would have been part of the usual international barter expected at peace conferences. As Hans J. Morgenthau has said, however, Wilson's program was studded with moral precepts. He found it impossible to compromise principles without abdicating his moral leadership. He had to pay a heavy price for having ignored European and Asiatic realities in proclaiming his peace program. Now there was nothing to do but to make the best of a bad situation.

As knowledge of Wilson's recession reached American shores, liberals were bewildered and dismayed. Compromise of principle did not fit into their tight frame of reference. Characteristically, these men were over-confident about big things—Utopia was a possibility, not a mere dream. They had had altogether too much faith that the European peoples, with the proper moral guidance, would sacrifice temporary benefits for enduring humanitarian gains. At the same time, they tended to be over-apprehensive about little things and equated concession to reality with wholesale betrayal.

The liberals had been reluctant to go to war. Simon-pure Darwinists, like Theodore Roosevelt, had believed war a natural part of the struggle for survival. Most of the liberals, however, were "reform" Darwinists who argued that it was man's duty to mitigate the harshness of nature by active steps. Some liberals had refused to follow Wilson to war. They had already prejudged the peace and were ready to enlighten fellow liberals who had decided to cast their lot with Wilson. None of them, moreover, had been happy warriors. They persuaded themselves that this was more than a war—it was the great opportunity for a new day for the world. Wilson, of course, had encouraged such unrealistic thinking. Taunted by pacifists for their acquiescence in the use of force, the Wilsonians took refuge in fond thoughts of peace. Eagerly they looked forward to the President's coming joust with the European reactionaries. When he was forced to compromise they were totally incapable of understanding his resort to expediency. He had destroyed their vision of a war-chastened world ready to turn over a brand new leaf. The President obviously was playing the ancient European game of diplomacy. This they could never forgive. To destroy him they were ready to make an unnatural alliance with his and their old enemies.

Of course not all of the liberals deserted. Some of them realized Wilson's predicament, accepted his solution, and fought valiantly for the League of Nations. It seems fair to say, however, that the majority of the politically independent liberals opposed both the treaty and its Siamese twin, the League. These independents were frequently theoretical internationalists. Their opposition to the treaty re-united them with liberals who had opposed the war and who were usually isolationists. This group in turn coalesced with the progressive-isolationists of the Borah–La Follette variety, who opposed any kind of international organization. The liberal front was thus considerably swollen by the influx of isolationist elements. The internationalists among them proclaimed loudly that they were not isolationists, but that they opposed this Covenant of the League of Nations. Such protests meant little for the net result was aid, comfort, and eventual victory for the great isolationist combine that was to frustrate Wilson's plans. . . .

In sum, it is apparent that the defection of the liberals helped defeat Wilson's league and unwittingly aided the creation of a new isolationism. The liberals had not been content to stand by. They joined the reactionary enemies of the President and made common cause with the progressive-isolationists with whom they shared many points of view. Circumstances brought theoretical internationalists such as Villard and Croly together with obdurate isolationists of the Borah–La Follette variety. Having helped to defeat the League by joining in the anti-Wilson combination, their own hopes for a new league were caught up in the isolationist groundswell. Versailles had separated the President from his liberal flank. He then had to depend upon partisan Democratic strength and a few loyal internationalists to carry his program. The same treaty that alienated the liberals, however, destroyed the unity of the Democratic party by unequal treatment of European nations and minorities. This had serious repercussions in America, a nation of immigrants.

* * *

The alienation of the hyphenates from Wilson and the Democratic party points up the importance of coincidence in history. The First World War marked the culmination of the great population shift from Europe to America. By this time there were millions of immigrants of the first and second generation in this country. The stirring events of the day revived ancient ties to European homelands and temporarily halted the weighty centripetal force of Americanization. The United States allied itself with one coalition of nations and made war upon another with the result of an accent upon hyphenization. There were now, as never before, Irish-Americans, German-Americans, Italian-Americans, and so on down the line. This emphasis increased as the European war stimulated the nationalist aspirations for independence of many subject peoples. Irishmen, Czechs, Poles, Latvians, Slavs, Hungarians, and other immigrant groups in America were stirred to action by the revolts of their parent nationalities. Each unit, incited by foreign agents, wanted the United States to stand godfather to the new states then in the making. But circumstances made it impossible for Wilson to deal equally with all these ambitions. He could, with equanimity, please the Poles whose reconstituted homeland had been wrested from the defeated nations and Bolshevist Russia. He could please the Jews by consenting to the Balfour Declaration for a Palestinian homeland because it happened to be sponsored by Britain. On the other hand, a strong stand for Irish self-determination would have meant a complete rupture with Lloyd George's government. Such a break the President could not risk.

The complete hostility of the German- and Austrian-Americans was also to be reckoned with. The war itself had already alienated most of them from Wilson and they became even more bitter when they learned of the harsh terms dealt to the vanquished in the treaties of peace. The President could afford no further nationalist defections. It was impossible, however, to please all of the splinter groups, for the good will of some could be bought only at the expense of displeasing others or, in some instances, by thwarting the territorial ambitions of land-hungry Allies.

There was more to the hyphenate revolt than resentment against the compromises on self-determination and the harsh terms of the peace. The second and third generations of immigrants were concerned more frequently with domestic rather than with foreign affairs. Until 1914, the cultural and intellectual leadership of the Old Americans had been taken for granted. Newcomers, to be sure, had found a place in the country, but they sat at the foot of the table. Their children had often been frustrated by social sneers and numerous obstacles which blocked the way up the ladder of success. Wartime prosperity had opened up new vistas to the "out" group of society, and as they pushed their way into bigger business, politics, and the professions, they demanded social equality. Some, at least, of the older stock Americans wanted to contest the challenge. Such people the immigrants identified with pro-British and pro-League groups because these movements were strong among the better people. Some of the hyphenates regarded the Scotch-Irish Wilson as one of their social enemies. The President did share the common conviction of the intellectual elite in regard to the superiority of Anglo-Saxon culture. He was also the leader of the pro-League Anglophiles, although he was less of a racist than Lodge or Beveridge. But the Republican opportunists had the best of the situation in spite of their previous records. As the "outs," they could wash their hands of direct responsibility for the war or for the peace. The emphasis of the G.O.P. on Americanism was welcome to immigrant ears despite its nativist overtones. For if nationality was something psychological rather than ethnic, it could be acquired. Newcomers saw a way of gaining increased status by capitalizing upon a fervid Americanism.

The Republicans grasped the situation. Circumstances had made it possible for them to split the internal unity of the Democrats, whose party had been nurtured on immigrant votes since the days of Jefferson. The hyphenate electorate, with some notable exceptions such as the Poles, was in their clutches. The next step was to amalgamate the new potential voters with the hard-core Republicans and the rabid nativists. Was there any other issue, besides hatred of Wilson and Versailles, that could unite the coalition and help close the yawning gap between reactionaries, hundred per cent Americans and fifty per cent hyphenates? By chance rather than design both the Republicans and the nascent isolationist coalition found a common denominator. All of the constituent groups were more or less anti-British. Twisting the lion's tail had long been standard political technique in the United States. It was time for a good hard wrench.

While the bulk of the Republicans did not hate England as did the German or Irish-Americans, they were nevertheless ready for a revolt against our partnership with the British in wartime. The Anglophiles had overreached themselves and now there was a Yankee rebound. This reaction came with sufficient force to congeal extraneous elements within the party. The pendulum was swinging back from the extreme pro-British posi-

tion. On its return trip it was picked up by Republican isolationists and pushed farther in the opposite direction. . . .

Reflection shows that never before in American history had Congress, state legislatures, and public opinion been so disturbed by hyphenate and nativist claims and countercharges. There was a babel of voices and a confusion of tongues. It began when Wilson stirred to hope and action a score of subject races and their American sympathizers. When he was unable to please all of them, his senatorial enemies invited the hyphenates to ride the nationalist train. They climbed aboard with alacrity, and in their enthusiasm, they blew the whistle long and hard. With their fellow-passengers, the nativists, they shouted that the roadbed of American history had been twisted and torn by Anglophiles and internationalists. Concurrently, the larger group of everyday unhyphenated Americans was ready to say: "A plague on all houses." They had sickened of both the noise of the hyphenate-patriots, and the internationalist clamor to make the world a better place for Europeans and Asiatics. Why not return to normality, let the foreigner fry in his own fat, and enjoy prosperity? "Deal us out," men said, of the game of world politics. Such sentiments were part of the deeper but more unspectacular ground-swell which pulled the American masses into the great isolationist undertow.

* * *

In the exuberant and confident days of 1918 the spirit of internationalism had captured the American mind. Slowly the skeptics rallied to undermine this attitude. At first there were only special interest groups—unremitting Republicans, disheartened liberals, flag-waving hundred percenters, and indignant hyphenates. For some time this alliance constituted a distinct minority. A war-weary people demanded a design for peace to compensate the world for the agony of strife. As it became apparent that it was difficult to translate ideals into reality, the isolationist combine became a majority. The sublimity of Wilson was to give way to the aridity of Harding and Coolidge.

The conventional reasons given for the retreat to isolationism are often more shallow than profound. It is commonplace to read that a senatorial cabal forced Wilson to accept either serious restrictions upon the Covenant or else outright defeat. The President refused to compromise and staked his program on the outcome of the 1920 presidential election. The Republicans won, so the contention continues, and decided to abandon the League. The outline of the story is correct as far as it goes. Such a superficial interpretation, however, begs the question. Had the American people really been persuaded that their own security demanded a collective formula for the world, no party could have permanently thwarted their desires. Mere political triumph does not explain the rejuvenation of Washington's Farewell Address. The majority of Americans, Republicans and Democrats alike, spurned Wilson's premise that peace was a seamless fabric. Popular opinions swung back to the older concept that American self-interest demanded a return to insulation from Old World political entanglements. Let us analyze the factors that reversed the internationalist tide.

The regression can be comprehended only in the light of the post-war spirit. Americans had soon wearied of saving the world. The trials and tribulations of war and the frustrations of peacemaking had dissipated the spell of idealism. Affairs in the wide world and at home seemed confused. The Bolshevist advance made the very word "international" suspect, and sent Americans scurrying to the shelter of traditional values. Unassimilated immigrants in city slums were blamed for economic heresies stemming from their European homelands. People came to feel that the only way to preserve order and property against the ideology of Lenin and Trotsky was to debar outside influences.

At the same time that men were drawing back from foreign contacts, they were enlarging their personal ambitions. Wartime prosperity had created a new and swollen middle class. Millions of people were anxious to relax their tensions and to enjoy their new status in old-fashioned tranquillity. Isolationism was part of the acute nostalgia for the good old days—for cigar store wooden Indians, for the *Police Gazette*, and for Casey who waltzed with a strawberry blonde. The impression was widespread that if we would shake off the responsibilities of the world, we could turn the clock back to a normality that had known no high costs of living, no income taxes, no small and oppressed nations, no grisly Reds, no thought of Article X or a League of Nations.

Americanism was the order of the day. Such sentiment was particularly strong among mature men who did so much of the talking and writing. Their impressionable years had been spent during the marvelous spurt of American economic power and prestige that came in the late nineteenth century. No other nation, certainly none in modern history, had achieved so much in such a short period of time. People gloried in the power of the United States and an innate selfishness made them reluctant to share our good fortune with other peoples. We should not, said one writer, trade the "Aladdin's lamp" of nationalism for "a newfangled contraption of a cheap, hastily constructed, foreign-made lamp of internationalism." Why forsake a protective tariff or an isolated foreign policy that had made possible such abundance? More perspicacious thinkers knew that the pre-war Old World stability was gone and that our long-run interests demanded that we lend a stout hand to the restoration of order. However, the masses were attracted to the simplest expedient which was to divorce ourselves from the turmoil of other peoples and watch the ramparts of the western hemisphere. . . .

Isolationists were able to capitalize on more than the mere abandonment of non-entanglement. There was a widespread notion that the League would cripple or destroy the Monroe Doctrine. For a full half century, exclusive American control of the western hemisphere had been welded to the older policy of isolationism. Now, it was argued, both would go to the scrap heap at the same time. To become one of the world's policemen was enough of a deviation from tradition. Did the League Covenant also mean that henceforth foreign nations would be the guardians of New World order? The question had been raised from the moment Wilson began to talk of collective security. While at Paris the President had been informed by leading Republican internationalists that if the Monroe Doctrine could be properly safeguarded the treaty would be "promptly ratified." At considerable cost to his own bargaining power at Versailles, Wilson had reopened the finished Covenant and had persuaded the powers to agree to the new Article XXI. This stipulated that nothing in the proposed arrangement would affect the validity of such "regional understandings" as the Monroe Doctrine. The language was necessarily ambiguous because no precise definition of the Doctrine could have pleased both the Senate and the rest of the world. Despite the nebulous concession, Wilson's enemies still said that the twin bases of our foreign policy were both to be sacrificed in one fateful leap in the dark. . . .

Linking the abandonment of the Monroe Doctrine to the end of non-entanglement posed a double-barreled threat to the foundations of American foreign policy. Many moderate internationalists hesitated to go that far, and while the moderates were reflecting, events played into the hands of the isolationists. The daily news from Europe made people shrink from further involvement at the expense of forsaking cherished policies. Time was on the side of the isolationists. A feeling of smugness, superiority, and safety behind our deep ocean moats was sweeping the country. . . .

Despite this manifest swing back to isolationism, there were many friends of the League left in the country and they held certain great advantages. A majority of the people wanted an association of nations of one kind or another. It was going to be difficult to keep America out of Wilson's league or a revamped substitute. To defeat this end the isolationist elements would have to coalesce and plan their strategy. Action on the treaty must be postponed until the hosts could gather together. The more time that could be gained, the more avenues of public opinion that could be turned against the League. The leadership and cadence came from the United States Senate. Isolationists in that august body supplied the generalship for the country-wide coalition. Not only did they defeat the treaty, but they also brought together strands of the new isolationism and nourished it till it won the hearts of the people. The activities of the senators and their allies are of prime importance in understanding the popular reversal from collective organization back to the isolationist tradition.

While liberal and hyphenate isolationists were important, they were specially oriented groups with limited representation in the Senate. Thus the most effective leadership in marshalling public opinion came from the blatant nationalists. Their arguments were couched in the appealing terms of Americanism. These senators both created and in turn reflected the mood of the country. Return to the policy of the Fathers, demanded the nationalists. Become Americans once more, they urged, and limit political questions to local concerns that we can understand and handle. America—great, self-sufficient, and refreshingly different—had no need for a League of Nations. In joining a world political body we had everything to lose and nothing to gain. Perplexed by continental disorders? they queried. Solve the problem by minding our own business. To Main Streeters, far more interested in the coming Dempsey-Willard fight than in Fiume or Danzig, this made sense. Nationalism, the nostalgic appeal to tradition, and the exaggerated fears of possible entanglements were arguments that struck the fancy of the common people. Mr. and Mrs. John Doe were becoming rapidly bored with the whole League business. They were shrinking back to their old lack of interest in and indifference to foreign affairs. The First World War had not brought the enduring conviction that a peaceful Europe was essential to American well-being.

The senatorial conclave that steered the fight against the League was, of course, headed by Lodge. In spite of the fact that the Massachusetts senator claimed to be a strong reservationist, his polished oratory supplied the extreme nationalists with many arguments against Wilson's plan. Lodge and his fellow reservationists insisted that only if America's hands were untied in future emergencies could she be of service to world peace and the welfare of mankind. Because the battle in the Senate chamber took most of Lodge's time, mustering the support of the country was left mostly to the admitted isolationists. William Edgar Borah was the original Irreconcilable, the leader of his self-styled "Battalion of Death." This band of fifteen equated compromise on the League question with treason. Borah not only commanded the die-hards in Washington, but also took upon himself the job of coordinating the nationwide isolationist coalition. His unique position in American politics made him precisely the right man for the job. Progressive in his own inconsistent way, he enjoyed the confidence of the liberals. At the same time he had not bolted to the Bull Moosers in 1912, and thus, in the eyes of the Old Guard, was innocent of that most heinous of American political crimes, party treachery. No other senator had such wide hyphenate connections. Yet despite his Irish and German associations, Borah's patriotic record was unassailable because, unlike so many of the other progressive-isolationist senators, he had voted for war. At that time he told Congress bluntly that he was joining no crusade nor sought any alliance but would fight only for his country and its rights. He called for the unconditional surrender of Germany dictated at the sword's point, and labeled all talk of world association "moral treason." Time and again Borah held Lodge and other reservationists from making any real concession to the pro-League forces. He insisted that the G.O.P. make no compromise with this "bolshevism" of world unity. Realizing the power of the press, Borah enlisted the invaluable aid of the magazine and newspaper tycoon, Frank A. Munsey, whose New York *Sun* was able to offset important pro-League papers in the big city. The senator told Munsey that if the people were informed of the real details of Wilson's proposal, the plan would be defeated by an avalanche of public indignation. Munsey did his best, supplied with plenty of information from Borah's office. The senator's indefatigable energy, wide connections, and enthusiasm wove together the various strands of isolationist thinking.

There can be little doubt of Borah's utter sincerity. His creed was simple and easy for the philistines to grasp: return to the teachings of Washington and foster "a strong national spirit, a national mind and purpose." Any friend of the League, he insisted, must admit that he was no longer willing to see the American flag above the banners of other nations. Like so many other senators, Borah was essentially old-fashioned, for he considered it unthinkable to abandon a policy that had so long insulated the United States from the vicissitudes of world turmoil. He was utterly impervious to the fact that changing concepts of space and economic entanglements had pushed America much closer to the European world. He could not comprehend that some new plan to keep the peace would have to replace the old balance of power. Borah was convinced of America's singular capacity to handle matters arising from Old

World instability when and if they impinged upon her own welfare. Hence the very idea of a League maintained by force looked like treachery designed only to betray the true interests of the country. The motives for this treason, to Borah's uncomplicated mind, seemed clear enough. Bankers, he thought, wanted the League in order to "gather their fruits from exploitation and investment." Desperately he wrote around the nation for documentary proof of this "sale of our country." When such evidence was not forthcoming, he interpreted the silence as meaning that the conspiracy was all the more subtle. Giving no ground to friend or foe, Borah carried the message of isolationism from Versailles to the Second World War. . . .

The Borah group won an immense victory when the Senate, on two separate occasions, voted down the treaty. The Republican leadership, under Lodge, had agreed upon fourteen reservations. Ten were of no great significance, because they merely clarified certain powers to be retained by the United States, that could hardly have been denied by ordinary interpretation of the Covenant. There were, however, four reservations that seriously imperiled Wilson's objectives. First of all, there was to be no obligation to act under the provisions of Article X without the specific approval of Congress in each question at issue. Thus any action by the League in preserving the peace was certain to be placed at the mercy of a congressional debate. Second, assent was withheld from the Shantung clause of the treaty, a step that would endanger Japanese support of the settlement. Third, the Monroe Doctrine was to be segregated from the League's scope of action, and the United States would refuse to arbitrate any dispute that impinged upon her traditional surveillance of New World security. Finally, we would not be obligated by a decision of the Council or Assembly where any one country (meaning the British Empire) had more than one vote, nor would we be bound by a decision to which we were a party if the nation pitted against us used more than one vote in obtaining the judgment.

The Irreconcilables played a masterful game of cards. They deliberately helped Lodge load these reservations on the treaty's back. Then when the treaty with addenda came before the Senate on November 19, 1919, Borah & Company voted with the Wilsonian Democrats against consent. On the question of the treaty as it stood, the Irreconcilables lined up with the Republican majority to vote nay. With four-fifths of the senators, puissant public opinion, and many organizations inclining toward the Covenant in one form or another, the issue was bound to rise once more. All attempts to reach a feasible compromise failed because the irresistible force of the President met the immovable object of the Republican high command. Thus, under virtually similar circumstances, the treaty failed once more in the Senate on March 19, 1920. More than a majority of the senators, but not the required two-thirds, voted for the League with reservations. Complete rejection of the League, even in the Senate, was not in 1920 the will of the majority. Time and events, however, were to play into the hands of the "Battalion of Death."

It is tempting to speculate what might have happened had a presidential election not been just around the corner. The internationalist spirit was still strong among cosmopolitan Republicans. Had Wilson's term not been at an end, it is conceivable that the Allied powers, anxious to launch the League with the United States a member, might have induced him to negotiate the entire matter. Had this occurred, the quickening of the League in Geneva might have revived waning American internationalism. All this, however, was not destined to be, for the isolationists were immensely strengthened by the campaign ballyhoo of the 1920 election. Wilson took the fatal step of asking the impossible—namely, that the election be "a great and solemn referendum" on the League. It would be difficult to imagine a more egregious error. The Republicans, who formed the ordinary majority, would be sure to pick up the President's gauntlet.

The merits of the League question aside, the Wilsonians would have had the odds heavily against them. Eight years of Democratic rule had built up the usual resentments against the party in power. To this must be added the jaded disillusionment against the war and its inconveniences which were bound to react against the "ins." Wilson, a competent political scientist, should have known that presidential elections are so intricate that it is impossible to fight them on any one issue. The League question could not be isolated and separated from the anti-Wilson political tide. As the President might well have anticipated had illness not blurred his foresight, the Republicans would not let the question be precipitated categorically. The G.O.P. could not afford to alienate their internationalist wing by an outright isolationist platform. Instead they straddled, compromised, overstated, and emotionalized the League issue. When the verdict was in, the Democrats had gone down to inglorious defeat. . . .

By March 4, 1921, when the florid

Harding rode up Pennsylvania Avenue with the peaked Wilson, the great isolationist front had been formed. The coalition contained many different types of active members. There were liberals who wanted no part of a League that had been fashioned by the turncoat Wilson. Communists gave active help to the isolationists because they regarded the League as a dangerous derelict lying in the path that led to the economic unity of mankind. Strangely enough, many immigrants were isolationists simply because of strong European attachments. Some of the victorious Republicans, especially those of the eastern seaboard, wanted an international organization, but opposed the League scheme in its existing form. Borah, Johnson, La Follette and their cohorts held tightly to a nineteenth-century form of nationalism, a concept which left no room for effective world organization. And there were the zealots who condemned everything foreign and who thought of our oceans as the Chinese had once thought of their wall. Important as all other factors were in evoking this mood of detachment, the nationalist creed was paramount. For that was a doctrine that immigrants and nativists, progressives and reactionaries, insular politicians and career diplomats had in common. Thus isolationism formed a common and seemingly solid ground amidst the drift of the twenties.

JOHN CHALMERS VINSON (1919–   ), professor
of history at the University of Georgia, has written
extensively on the Senate's role in shaping American
foreign policy. *The Parchment Peace: the United
States Senate and the Washington Conference,
1921–1922* (1955) and *William E. Borah and the
Outlawry of War* (1957) are two of his earlier
contributions. In his most recent book, *Referendum
for Isolation*, he examines the arguments for and
against Article 10 of the League Covenant.
These arguments, he maintains, reveal fundamental
differences of opinion that could not be reconciled.
The final clash of opinion came in the election of 1920,
in which the fight centered on Article 10.*

▶ # *The Election of 1920:*
A Referendum for Isolation

In retrospect it is clear that America's final rejection of Article Ten, as well as the balance of the League of Nations Covenant, came November 2, 1920, with the landslide election of Harding to the presidency. It is generally held, however, that this decision was not the result of a conscious choice by the voters; that it was not the "solemn referendum" that Wilson hoped it would be. The decision really came during the next four years as the victorious Republican administration equivocated and evaded the issue of world organization until popular interest became apathetic. Of course the presidential election, as always, involved many conflicting issues of domestic politics, making it impossible to say with certainty that a vote for Harding was a vote against the League. For one thing, if the League had been considered the paramount issue, it is argued, Harding's speeches were too indefinite to show where he stood. For another, the voters, bored with eighteen months of debate, were indifferent to the League as a campaign issue.

Further confusion resulted from attempts to determine the actual ability of the candidates to carry out in terms of practical politics their campaign promises. Assuming that Harding was opposed to the League, it was argued that he would be forced to accept it after election in order to conciliate the Hughes-Root-Taft wing of the party. Cox, although for the Wilson League, could never as President drive it through

---

* From John Chalmers Vinson, *Referendum for Isolation, Defeat of Article Ten of the League
of Nations Covenant* (Athens, Ga.: The University of Georgia Press, 1961), pp. 110–120.

a Senate in which more than a third opposed Article Ten. His election would mean nothing more than a continuation of the stalemate between President and Senate. . . .

From the amorphous oratory of the campaign emerged startlingly stark and definite opinions on Article Ten. This one of the Covenant's twenty-six Articles was singled out and condemned, for reasons of political expediency as well as principle, by all important factions of the Republican party. It was denounced with a finality seldom employed in elections except to excoriate the prevalence of sin in the opposing administration.

There was a general recognition of vast difference between a League with Article Ten and a League without that provision, the difference being between terminating traditional policies of non-entanglement and continuing those policies, between unending responsible involvement in European politics and complete freedom of choice in foreign policy. The positive qualities of a League without Article Ten were not defined during the campaign, but the negative features of the mutual guarantee were made unmistakably clear.

Harding, for all of his skillful obfuscation of issues, with the hearty approval of the irreconcilables spoke out clearly against the mutual guarantee. The so-called pro-League wing of the Republican party publicly and emphatically declared its rejection of Article Ten in the widely published Appeal of the Thirty-One. This rejection was made even more final when two of the faction's most respected and best informed leaders, Root and Hughes, strongly condemned Article Ten many times in speeches during the closing days of the campaign.

In the Democratic camp there was more of a struggle over the Article. Cox and Roosevelt sought to stand by Wilson's program for immediate ratification without crippling reservations. But the party platform did not preclude reservations making American obligations clearer and more specific. As the campaign neared its end, Cox placed more and more emphasis on this escape clause, giving the impression that he would accept sweeping changes to Article Ten. Alarmed Republicans feared he would soon run on their platform. Certainly it was not clear that a vote for Cox in November was a vote for an unreserved and unmodified Article Ten.

The Republican party at its National Convention had called once again on the "shrewd mind and cunning hand" of Elihu Root to frame a statement on the League in general on which its friends and enemies within the party could unite. Despite Root's magnificent effort to please all factions the battle for control of the candidate continued. The campaign speeches of Harding indicated a movement away from the League and toward a wholly different organization designated as an association of nations. Conceived in August with the aid of George Harvey and Richard Washburn Child, the association of nations drew the conflicting statements of Harding into a complicated and ambiguous plan for international cooperation designed as a straddle enabling Harding to placate the irreconcilables, who wanted no league, and the liberals, who wished to join the League. In short, he promised at this time to work with the "best minds" in the country after his election in order to establish "a society of free nations . . . so organized as to make attainment of peace a reasonable possibility." Later in the campaign Harding was pushed into the irreconcilable camp to keep Brandegee and Johnson from bolting the party. Harding soon realized that "This issue . . . does not present to the American people the question whether they shall favor some form of association among the nations for the purpose of preserving international peace, but whether they favor the particular League proposed by President Wilson. . . . The obligations are clear enough and specific enough. I oppose the League not because I fail to understand . . . 'What we are being let in for,' but because I believe I understand precisely 'what we are being let in for.'

"I do not want to clarify these obligations; I want to turn my back on them. It is not interpretation but rejection, that I am seeking. My position is that the present league strikes a deadly blow at our constitutional integrity and surrenders to a dangerous extent our independence of action. . . .

"The issue therefore is clear. I understand the position of the Democratic candidate and he understands mine. . . . It is that he favors going into the Paris League and I favor staying out. . . . We shall have an association of nations for the promotion of international peace, but one which shall so definitely safeguard our sovereignty and recognize our ultimate and unmortgaged freedom of action. . . . that it will have back of it the united support of the American people."

On Article Ten Harding was even more clear and specific. He described Article Ten as "not only the most dangerous provision in the Covenant, but, in its sinister possibilities, it is the most dangerous proposition ever presented to the American people." With words of "utmost precision" the Article bound America to "an obligation which under certain easily foreseeable circumstances will require the use of armed forces. It is true that the Constitution invests Congress with the sole power to declare war, but if war shall become necessary in order to fulfill this or any other treaty provision Congress must either declare war or repudiate the obligation. Let no one be deceived; the choice would be between two things—war and dishonor." Nevertheless, Harding favored a league provided the United States was required to act only in accord with the "test of righteousness" and assume no other obligation. A few days later, Harding asserted that Article Ten was indeed the "heart of the League" as Wilson had asserted. "I know it is the heart of the League,—the steel heart, hidden beneath a coat of mail. Article 10 creates a world government, puts America in alliance with four great powers to rule the world by force of arms and commits America to give her sons for all the battlefields of the Old World. . . ."

Early in October the Democrats launched a campaign to have the text of the Covenant published as widely as possible. The Chairman of the Democratic National Committee, George White, asked Will Hays to enlist the cooperation of Republican newspapers for such a program "in the interest of truth which the righteous certainly have no reason to fear. . . ." The Republican party was cool to the suggestion. At the same time the party leadership did not wish to be pushed to a definite position against the League. To counteract the reluctance to take a stand, Hays enlisted once again the services of Elihu Root. They raised, with the aid of Jacob Gould Schurman, Paul D. Cravath, and George Wickersham, a standard to which pro-League Republicans might rally. To add greater luster their argument was signed by thirty-one leading

Republicans, including "seventeen college presidents and executives."

The Appeal of the Thirty-one (the name afterwards given the document) was remarkable even as campaign literature. It was accepted as a firm approval "for the League of Nations in the form in which it had been endorsed by the League to Enforce Peace," to quote Hays. Yet nowhere in the document was any such statement made; "the" League was referred to only as "the proposed agreement." While support for "a" league was offered, the closest approach to endorsement of "the" League was the statement: "We therefore believe that we can effectively advance the cause of international co-operation to promote peace by supporting Mr. Harding. . . ."

So vague was the actual text that it inspired many interpretations. The *New York Times*, for example, deduced that the proposal advocated taking the best features from the League Covenant and combining them with Root's plan for an international court. The finished creation, it was inferred, would be an entirely new organization, an association of nations.

Even if the signees had advocated adherence to the League of Nations, there was little possibility that they could have executed their pledge. As President H. N. McCracken of Vassar said in refusing to sign the appeal, "The names of those signing it will not in my opinion have influence on Senator Harding's foreign policy after the election."

All of this might have been apparent to any other careful reader of the Appeal. But there were few careful readers, and there were many voters who wanted to be assured that they could support the League and Harding. The statement was accepted by the public as a full endorsement of a modified League

by men who would make the foreign policy of the Republican administration. Chairman Hays, on the one hand, and candidate Cox, on the other, agreed that the Appeal influenced thousands of wavering Republicans to vote for Harding.

The change of votes did not decide the election by any means. The Appeal, however, was especially significant in the history of Article Ten. For all of its vagueness as to the League of Nations, the Appeal was remarkably clear and specific in its renunciation of Article Ten. It called in unequivocal language for the elimination of Article Ten from any peace plan considered by the United States and the establishment of a legal tribunal resting on the enforcing power of public opinion.

The Thirty-one acknowledged that Wilson believed Article Ten to be the "heart of the League." They then attacked the Article with the same arguments the most irreconcilable Senate opponents had employed. Article Ten, the statement asserted, obligated all members "to go to war whenever war may be necessary to preserve the territorial integrity or political independence of any member of the League against external aggression." The Thirty-one recommended "that the true course to bring Americans into an effective league to preserve peace is not by insisting with Mr. Cox upon the acceptance of such a provision as Article X . . . but by frankly calling upon the other nations to agree to changes in the proposed agreement which will obviate this vital objection." To accomplish this aim "we can look only to the Republican Party and its candidate; the Democratic Party and Mr. Cox are not bound to follow it."

Actually, the statement did little to clarify and much to confuse the issue at the time. It did help create the impression (as Root, its principal author, had hoped) that the real issue was the Wilson League, based on force, versus an "Americanized" league, based on law. Furthermore, Root philosophized, leagues in the popular mind were synonymous with peace, and so it was expedient for Republicans during the campaign to advocate some sort of league in order to attract the vote of "clergymen, women, and other good people." . . .

Another prominent signer of the Appeal of the Thirty-one, Charles Evans Hughes, was more explicit in condemning Article Ten. He asserted, in a speech in New Haven, October 23: "We desire to have the obligation of Article X nullified, for it has no place in a proper covenant for an association of nations to promote peace." In great detail Hughes explained that Wilson in his interpretative reservations to Article Ten had never touched this central issue—America's obligation to act. Wilson insisted upon Article Ten "because it does impose an obligation and because he desires the United States to rest under that obligation." That was why Wilson would not accept the Lodge reservation, for the point of that reservation, declared Hughes, "is that it denies the obligation itself." Cox, too, in announcing his willingness to accept modifications to Article Ten was not prepared to nullify the obligation it imposed. The real and only issue of the campaign, Hughes insisted, was Article Ten. The Republicans were against "the obligation as one which we cannot assume in accordance with the principles of our institutions." Hughes was completely honest and consistent in his abhorrence to the obligations of Article Ten, as he was to demonstrate so many times during the next

four years as secretary of state. It is difficult to argue that he did not read the sentiment of the American people with great accuracy.

In a political campaign ideas of great impact must be expressed in simple terms. The election was a vote for peace or war, said the *New York Times*. Candidate Cox declared that it was a simple question of "the gospel of Cain against the gospel of Christ." Thus the League meant peace; a vote against it meant war. But this easily comprehended idea was clouded by the Republican attack on Article Ten. A league meant peace; Article Ten meant war. The force of this argument had impressed many Democrats—so many in fact that the party platform was not the unreserved endorsement for the League that Wilson wished, but was tempered by the agreement to accept helpful reservations. Early in October, Governor Cox announced that he favored a reservation to Article Ten stating that the United States would not assume an obligation to defend other members of the League "unless approved and authorized by Congress in each case." Such a change could mean that the moral force of the guarantee against aggression would be seriously impaired if not completely eliminated. Cox gave no specific interpretation of the reservation, but he did deny publicly Root's charge that he would "insist upon the Treaty just as Mr. Wilson negotiated it." He went on to say, "I will accept reservations that will clarify, that will be helpful, that will reassure the American people, and that as a matter of good faith will clearly state to our associates in the League that Congress and Congress alone has the right to declare war, and that our Constitution sets up limits in legislation or treaty-making beyond which we can not go." Any reservations from any source, Cox added, would be carefully considered provided they were proffered in the spirit of sincerity and helpfulness. If elected he promised to sit down and consider the League with the members of the Senate, with Wilson, with Root, with Taft, and with all other sincere friends of the Treaty.

These were campaign statements and might mean much or little. Generally they were interpreted as meaning that Cox was weakening his advocacy of Article Ten. The New York Times expressed some surprise that Wilson was willing to endorse Cox's work in a letter published just before the election. Elsewhere Cox's advocacy of the League was denounced as uninformed and ineffectual. The New Republic declared Article Ten to be dead even before the election. Cox had repudiated it and no Republican faction favored the Article.

There was poignant symbolism in Wilson's first speech in over a year, delivered at the close of the campaign. Seated in a wheel chair and speaking in a voice barely audible, Wilson declared that unless Article Ten was honored, the League would be virtually worthless. Article Ten, he continued, assured the world that a future aggressor would not run rampant as Germany had done in 1914. It was "the specific redemption of the pledge which the free governments of the world gave to their people when they entered the war." In America, however, the pledge had been repudiated even before the speech was made. The revolution in American foreign policy, like its leader, was mortally ill. Few who went to the polls heeded the message of the broken old man in the White House.

Contemporary observers were not all willing to accept the verdict of the Nation that the discussions on the League during the campaign were "almost 100 per cent flapdoodle." The issue, noted the Literary Digest, was one "that would not down" and "it is upon Article X that the fight centers at the last." It was "the pith of the controversy." The pro-League Philadelphia Public Ledger, even before the election, concluded that the American people would not accept a covenant containing Article Ten. Only "an exceedingly poor student of political psychology" would cherish any hope that Article Ten could be put through the Senate in the next two years. The New Republic agreed but believed that "behind the Senate Republicans there was a profound popular instinct against the character of the peace," and an unwillingness to enforce the Treaty of Versailles by force of arms. This opinion was confirmed to the satisfaction of the editor by the results of the election. The people were overwhelmingly against Article Ten.

The result of the election was, no doubt, too one-sided to be ascribed to any one cause more definite than "a mighty wave of protest." As for the League, the results frequently were interpreted to suit the hopes of the interpreter. Hiram Johnson, on the one hand, was sure the issue in the election had been the League and "no amount of sophistry or pretense" could obscure the fact that "the menacing, dangerous, and entangling league has been emphatically and overwhelmingly repudiated." Herbert Hoover, on the other hand, asserted that "the vote as a whole" was "distinctly in favor of the participation of the United States in some form of international agreement for the maintenance of peace." To a marked degree the real problem was simply one of semantics. Judging by the campaign statements and considering the record of events during the next two decades, it is safe to say that the people had repudiated Article Ten. Taft probably outlined in his post-election statement the most advanced type of international organization that Americans would have accepted. The organization, which he was sure Harding would establish soon, would center "around an international court, with teeth in it." Article Ten "of course, must be eliminated if the United States is to enter a league." Otherwise the ground-plan, or organization, of the present League, improved by amendments, would fulfill Harding's aim.

The fight in 1920 centered on Article Ten and it was consciously and emphatically eliminated from any plans for American participation in international organizations. The one theory on which Wilson had built his whole League program was dead. The idea of a league still had popular appeal but only to the degree that commitments and obligations were eliminated. The Wilson League was dead in the United States. What the Harding association of nations could do with the United States as a free agent whose "only interest and commitment would be to the peace of the world" remained to be seen.

Today's survey textbook account of the League fight is, at least in its general outline, derived largely from the two books on the subject by THOMAS A. BAILEY (1902–   ). Bailey, like Haynes, Fleming, and Holt, praises Wilson's vision of collective security, but, unlike these writers, he puts most of the blame on Wilson and his docile followers for the failure to get the League approved. Bailey, one of the country's foremost diplomatic historians, is Byrne Professor of History at Stanford University. In addition to his many monographs and articles, he has written a study of the impact of public opinion on American foreign policy and an extremely popular textbook on diplomatic history.*

▶ ## *Wilson to Blame for Failure of the League*

The treaty was now dead, as far as America was concerned. Who had killed it?

The vital role of the loyal Democrats must be reemphasized. If all of them who professed to want the treaty had voted "Yea," it would have passed with more than a dozen votes to spare. If the strait-jacket of party loyalty had not been involved, the necessary two-thirds could easily have been mustered.

In the previous November, the Democrats might have voted against the treaty (as they did) even without White House pressure. But this time [in March] pressure had to be applied to force them into line, and even in the face of Wilsonian wrath almost half of them bolted. On the day of the final balloting the newsmen observed that

two Cabinet members (Burleson and Daniels), possibly acting at the President's direction, were on the floor of the Senate, buttonholing waverers. The day after the fateful voting Hitchcock wrote Wilson that it had required the "most energetic efforts" on his part *to prevent a majority of the Democrats from surrendering to Lodge.*

Desertion of the President . . . is no light offense in the political world, especially when he has declared himself emphatically. Senators do not ordinarily court political suicide. Wilson still had the patronage bludgeon in his hands, and having more than a trace of vindictiveness, he could oppose renegade senators when they ran again, and in fact did so.

Many of the loyal Democrats were

---

*Reprinted with permission of The Macmillan Company from *Woodrow Wilson and the Great Betrayal* by Thomas A. Bailey, pp. 271–282, 285–287. Copyright 1945 by Thomas A. Bailey.

up for reelection in 1920. They certainly were aware of the effects of party treachery on their political fortunes. They knew—or many of them knew—that they were killing the treaty; they made no real effort to revive it; they must have wanted it killed—at least until after the November election.

One striking fact stands out like a lighthouse. With the exception of Hitchcock of Nebraska, Johnson of South Dakota, and Thomas of Colorado, *every single one of the twenty-three senators who stood loyally with Wilson in March came from south of the Mason and Dixon line.* Only four of the "disloyal" twenty-one represented states that had seceded in 1860–1861. At the polls, as well as on the floor of the Senate, decent southern Democrats voted "the way their fathers shot." As between bothersome world responsibility on the one hand, and loyalty to President, party, section, and race on the other, there was but one choice. Perhaps world leadership would come eventually anyhow.

Democratic senators like Walsh of Montana and Ashurst of Arizona were not from the South. When the issue was clearly drawn between loyalty to party and loyalty to country, their consciences bade them choose the greater good. Ashurst had gone down the line in supporting Wilson; but several days before the final vote he declared, "I am just as much opposed to a White House irreconcilable as I am to a Lodge irreconcilable."

A word now about public opinion.

In March [1920], as in November [1919], more than 80 per cent of the senators professed to favor the treaty with some kind of reservations. All the polls and other studies indicate that this was roughly the sentiment of the country. Yet the senators were unable to scrape together a two-thirds vote for any one set of reservations.

The reaction of many newspaper editors, as before, was to cry out against the shame of it all—this indictment of the "capacity of our democracy to do business." We had astonished the world by our ability to make war; we now astonished the world with our "imbecility" in trying to make peace. How could we blame other countries for thinking us "a nation of boobs and bigots"? The Louisville *Courier-Journal* (Democrat), referring to our broken promises to the Allies, cried that we stood betrayed as "cravens and crooks," "hypocrites and liars."

Partisan Republican newspapers loudly blamed the stiff-backed Wilson and his "me-too" senators. Two wings of "irreconcilables"—the Wilsonites and the "bitter-enders"—had closed in to execute a successful pincers movement against the treaty. The New York *Tribune* (Independent Republican) condemned the "inefficiency, all-sufficiency and self-sufficiency of our self-named only negotiator," Woodrow Wilson. If the treaty died, said the *Tribune,* the handle of the dagger that pierced its heart would bear the "initials 'W. W.' "

If Republicans scolded Democrats, Democrats scolded Republicans. Lodge and his cheap political tricks were roundly condemned, and the general conclusion was that "the blood of the Treaty stains the floor of the Republican wigwam." A few of the less partisan Democratic journals openly conceded that Wilson's obstinacy had something to do with the final result. William Jennings Bryan asserted from the platform that this "most colossal crime against our nation and the civilized world in all history" made his "blood boil." He began a vigorous campaign against the two-thirds rule in the Senate. "A majority of Congress can declare war," he cried; "it ought to be as easy to end a war as to begin it."

The leading liberal journals, as before, were sadly happy. They rejoiced that the result would clear the way for a renovation of the treaty, but they regretted that the pact had been defeated as a result of partisanship rather than as a result of the betrayal of Wilson's promises.

An impressive number of the more discerning editors deplored the fact that the issue was now in the dirty hands of politicians. An electoral referendum, it was felt, would merely confuse the issue; such a canvass could not possibly reveal anything more than was already known, namely, that *an overwhelming majority of the people wanted the treaty with some kind of reservations.*

Is it true that the invalid in the White House really strangled the treaty to death with his own enfeebled hands?

It is seldom that statesmen have a second chance—a second guess. They decide on a course of action, and the swift current of events bears them downstream from the starting point. Only rarely does the stream reverse itself and carry them back.

In November, Wilson had decided that he wanted deadlock, because he reasoned that deadlock would arouse public opinion and force the Senate to do his bidding. The tidal wave of public opinion did surge in, and Wilson got his second chance. But he threw it away, first by spurning compromise (except on his terms), and then by spurning the Lodge reservations.

There had been much more justification for Wilson's course in November

than in March. In November he was sick, secluded, was fed censored news, and was convinced by Hitchcock that the strategy of deadlock was sound. In March, he was much improved in health, far less secluded, more in touch with the press and with the currents of opinion, though probably still not enough. He consulted even less with the Senate, presumably because he had made up his mind in advance to oppose the Lodge reservations. In November, there was a fair possibility of reconsideration; in March, it was clear that the only possibility lay in making the League an issue in the coming campaign. Wilson, with his broad knowledge of government and politics, should have seen that this hope was largely if not completely illusory. Perhaps he would have seen it had he not been blinded by his feeling for Lodge.

The evidence is convincing that Wilson wanted the issue cast into the hurly-burly of politics. He could not accept Lodge's terms; Lodge would not accept his terms. The only possible chance of beating the senator—and this was slim indeed—was to win a resounding mandate in 1920.

Yet this strategy . . . meant further delay. At Paris, the feeling at times had been, "Better a bad treaty today than a good treaty four months hence." Europe was still in chaos, and increasingly in need of America's helping hand. Well might the Europeans cry, "Better a treaty with the Lodge reservations today than a probable treaty without reservations after the election." Or as Dr. Frank Crane wrote in *Current Opinion,* "It is vastly more needful that some sort of League be formed, *any sort,* than that it be formed *perfectly.*" (Italics Crane's.)

Yet Wilson, for the reasons indicated, could not see all this clearly. Four days after the fatal vote he wrote Hitchcock, praising him for having done all in his power to protect the honor of the nation and the peace of the world against the Republican majority.

Mrs. Wilson, no doubt reflecting her husband's views, later wrote, "My conviction is that Mr. Lodge put the world back fifty years, and that at his door lies the wreckage of human hopes and the peril to human lives that afflict mankind today."

To the very end Wilson was a fighter. When the Scotch-Irish in him became aroused, he would nail his colors to the mast. He said in 1916 that he was "playing for the verdict of mankind." His conception of duty as he saw it was overpowering. He once remarked that if he were a judge, and it became his duty to sentence his own brother to the gallows, he would do so—and afterwards die of a broken heart.

It is well to have principles; it is well to have a noble conception of duty. But Wilson, as he became warmed up in a fight, tended to get things out of focus and to lose a proper sense of values.

The basic issue in 1920 was the Hitchcock reservations or the Lodge reservations. Wilson accepted those of Hitchcock while rejecting those of Lodge, which, he said, completely nullified the treaty and betrayed his promises to the Allies and to the American dead.

This . . . was a gross exaggeration. Minds no less acute than Wilson's, and less clouded with sickness and pride, denied that the Lodge reservations completely nullified the treaty. To the man in the street—in so far as he gave the dispute thought—there was little discernible difference between the two sets of reservations. How could one decry statements which merely reaffirmed the basic principles of the Constitution and of our foreign policy? To a vast number of Americans the Lodge reservations, far from nullifying the treaty, actually improved it. This was so apparent to even the most loyal Democrats in the Senate that Wilson could barely keep them in line.

In the final analysis the treaty was slain in the house of its friends rather than in the house of its enemies. In the final analysis it was not the two-thirds rule, or the "irreconcilables," or Lodge, or the "strong" and "mild reservationists," but Wilson and his docile following who delivered the fatal stab. If the President had been permitted to vote he would have sided with Borah, Brandegee, Johnson, and the other "bitter-enders"—though for entirely different reasons.

Wilson had said that the reservation to Article X was a knife thrust at the heart of the Covenant. Ironically, he parried this knife thrust, and stuck his own dagger, not into the heart of the Covenant, but into the entire treaty.

This was the supreme act of infanticide. With his own sickly hands Wilson slew his own brain child—or the one to which he had contributed so much.

This was the supreme paradox. He who had forced the Allies to write the League into the treaty, unwrote it; he who had done more than any other man to make the Covenant, unmade it —at least so far as America was concerned. And by his action, he contributed powerfully to the ultimate undoing of the League, and with it the high hopes of himself and mankind for an organization to prevent World War II.

The preceding dogmatic observations are of course qualified by the phrase, "in the last analysis."

Many elements enter into a log jam. Among them are the width of the stream, the depth of the stream, the swiftness of the current, the presence of boulders, the size of the logs, and the absence of enough lumberjacks. No one of these factors can be solely responsible for the pile-up.

Many elements entered into the legislative log jam of March, 1920. Among them were isolationism, partisanship, senatorial prerogative, confusion, apathy, personal pride, and private feuds. No one of them was solely responsible for the pile-up. *But as the pile-up finally developed, there was only one lumberjack who could break it, and that was Woodrow Wilson.* If at any time before the final vote he had told the Senate Democrats to support the treaty with the Lodge reservations, or even if he had merely told them that they were on their own, the pact would almost certainly have been approved. So "in the last analysis" the primary responsibility for the failure in March rested with Wilson.

What about Lodge? If the treaty would have passed by Wilson's surrendering, is it not equally true that it would have passed by Lodge's surrendering?

The answer is probably "Yes," but the important point is that Lodge had far less responsibility for getting the treaty through than Wilson. If Lodge had yielded, he probably would have created a schism within his ranks. His ultimate responsibility was to keep the party from breaking to pieces, and in this he succeeded. Wilson's ultimate responsibility was to get the treaty ratified, and in this he failed. With Lodge, as with any truly partisan leader, the party comes before country; with the President the country should come before party, though unhappily it often does not.

It is possible that Wilson saw all this—but not clearly enough. He might have been willing to compromise if his adversary had been any other than Lodge. But so bitter was the feeling between the two men that Wilson, rather than give way, grasped at the straw of the election of 1920.

Lodge did not like Wilson either, but he made more of a show of compromising than the President. He actually supported and drove through amendments to his original reservations which were in line with Wilson's wishes, and he probably would have gone further had the "irreconcilables" not been on his back. He fought the crippling Irish reservation, as well as others supported by the "bitter-enders." Finally, he gave the Democrats a fair chance to reconsider their vote and get on the bandwagon, but they spurned it.

If Lodge's words mean anything, and if his actions were not those of a monstrous hypocrite, he actually tried to get the treaty through with his reservations. When he found that he could not, he washed his hands of the whole business in disgust.

The charge is frequently made that, if Wilson had yielded to his adversary, Lodge would have gleefully piled on more reservations until Wilson, further humiliated, would have had to throw out the whole thing.

The strongest evidence for this view is a circumstantial story which Secretary [of Agriculture] Houston relates. During a Cabinet meeting Wilson was called to the telephone, and agreed to make certain concessions agreeable to Lodge. Before adjournment the telephone rang again, and word came that Lodge would not adhere to his original proposal.

This story is highly improbable, because Wilson attended no Cabinet meetings between September 2, 1919, and April 13, 1920. By the latter date, all serious attempts at compromise had been dropped; by the earlier date the treaty was still before the Senate committee, and the Lodge reservations, though in an embryonic stage, were yet unborn. But, even if the story is true, it merely proves that Lodge veered about, as he frequently did under "irreconcilable" pressure.

In March, as in November, all Wilson had to do was to send over Postmaster General Burleson to the Senate a few minutes before the final vote with the quiet word that the Democrats were to vote "Yea." The treaty would then have passed with the Lodge reservations, and Lodge could hardly have dared incur for himself or his party the odium of moving to reconsider for the purpose of screwing on more reservations. Had he tried to do so, the "mild reservationists" almost certainly would have blocked him.

A few days after the disastrous final vote, Wilson's only comment to Tumulty was, "They have shamed us in the eyes of the world." If his previous words said what he really meant, he was hardly more shamed by the defeat of the treaty than by the addition of the Lodge reservations. In his eyes it all amounted to the same thing.

If the treaty had passed, would the President have been willing to go through with the exchange of ratifications? Would he not have pocketed it, as he threatened to do prior to the November vote?

Again, if Wilson's words may be taken at their face value, this is what he would have done. He had not backed down from his pre-November

position. His Jackson Day message and his letter to Hitchcock made it unmistakably clear that he preferred the uncertainties of a political campaign to the certainties of ratification with the Lodge reservations. The addition of the indefensible Irish reservation provided even stronger justification for pocketing the entire pact.

It is probable that some of the loyal Democrats voted as they did partly because they were convinced that Wilson was going to pigeonhole the treaty anyhow. From their point of view it was better that the odium for defeat should seemingly rest on Lodge rather than on their President. It also seems clear that Wilson preferred, as in November, to have the blood of the treaty on the Senate doorstep rather than on his. As he wrote to Secretary [of State] Colby, on April 2, 1920, the slain pact lay heavily on the consciences of those who had stabbed it, and he was quite willing to have it lie there until those consciences were either awakened or crushed.

Yet it is one thing to say, just before Senate action, "I will pocket the treaty." It is another, after the pact is approved and sent to the White House, to assume this tremendous responsibility. The eyes of the world are upon the President; he is the only man keeping the nation out of the peace which it so urgently needs; he is the one man standing in the way of the rehabilitation which the world so desperately demands. Public pressure to ratify in such a case would be enormous—probably irresistible.

Some years later Senator Hitchock said that in the event of senatorial approval Wilson would possibly have waited for the November election. If he had won, he would have worked for the removal of the Lodge reservations; if he had lost, then the compulsion to go through with ratification would have become overpowering. By November more than six months would have passed, and by that time Wilson might have developed a saner perspective.

But this is all speculation. Wilson gave orders that the treaty was to be killed in the Senate chamber. And there it died.

One other line of inquiry must be briefly pursued. Is it true, as some writers allege, that the thirty-odd Allied signatories of the original treaty would have rejected the Lodge reservations when officially presented? We recall that under the terms of the preamble these nations were privileged to acquiesce silently or file objections.

One will never know the answer to this question, because Wilson denied the other signatories a chance to act. But it seems proper to point to certain probabilities.

One or more of the Latin American nations might have objected to the reservation regarding the then hated Monroe Doctrine. Yet the Monroe Doctrine would have continued to exist anyhow; it was already in the Covenant; and these neighboring republics might well have swallowed their pride in the interest of world peace.

Italy probably would have acquiesced, and the evidence is strong that France would have done likewise. The Japanese could not completely overlook the Shantung reservation, but it was generally recognized in their press as meaningless, and for this reason it might have been tolerated, though not without some loss of face. It is noteworthy that the most important Japanese newspapers regretted the Senate stalemate as an encouragement to world instability, particularly in China.

Great Britain probably would have been the chief objector. The reservation on Ireland was highly offensive but completely innocuous, for the British lion had long endured Irish-American tail-twistings in pained but dignified silence. The reservation on six-to-one was a slap at the loyal and sacrificing Dominions, but it did not mean that their vote was to be taken away. Moreover, the contingency envisaged by this proviso was unlikely to arise very often, and in the long run would doubtless have proved inconsequential.

In sum, there were only two or three reservations to which the outside powers could seriously object. If they had objected, it is probable that a satisfactory adjustment could have been threshed out through diplomatic channels. For when it became clear that only a few phrases stood between the United States and peace, the dictates of common sense and the pressure of public opinion probably would have led to an acceptable compromise. If the Senate had refused to give ground in such a case, then the onus would have been clearly on it and not on Wilson. . . .

One final question. Who won after all these months of parliamentary jockeying?

Lodge the master parliamentarian had not won—that is, if he really wanted the treaty with his reservations. As in November, he was unable to keep the "irreconcilables" in line on the crucial vote, and he was unable to muster a two-thirds majority. He finally had to confess failure of leadership, except in so far as he prevented a schism.

The Republican party had not won. Lodge had avoided a serious split with the "bitter-enders" by knuckling under when they laid down the law. But the

Republican leaders did not really want the issue in the campaign, and they had made strong efforts to keep it out. Now it was on their hands to cause them no end of embarrassment.

Wilson had not won. He has been praised for having kept the party ranks intact, and for having retained undisputed leadership of his following. But the Democrats in the Senate split 21 for the treaty to 23 against it, and that is hardly holding one's followers in line. Wilson lost irreparably because he did not get his treaty, even with reservations, and because he was doomed to lose again by insisting on a referendum where there could be no referendum.

The Democrats had not won. The treaty issue had caused a serious rift in the Senate, and Bryan, who was still a great leader, was on the rampage. Except for Wilson and some of his "yes men," there were few Democratic leaders who wanted this troublesome issue catapulted into the campaign. Yet there it was.

The United States had not won. It had won the war, to be sure; but it was now kicking the fruits of the victory back under the peace table. We had helped turn Europe into a scrap heap, and now we were scrapping the treaty. We were going to stand by the Allies—with our arms folded. We were throwing away the only hope of averting World War II.

The real victor was international anarchy.

ALEXANDER L. GEORGE (1920–   ) is a senior staff member of The RAND Corporation and former head of its Social Science Department. During World War II he served as a political analyst in the Office of Strategic Services. Much of his work involved the interpretation of foreign propaganda which, at base, was a problem in content analysis of psychological warfare. He subsequently received his Ph.D. in political science at the University of Chicago and since then has written numerous articles and one book on propaganda analysis. His wife, JULIETTE L. GEORGE, has an M.A. in sociology from Columbia University, and she too was a government analyst of propaganda during the war. In their biography of Wilson and Colonel House, they suggest a provocative psychanalytical explanation for Wilson's refusal to compromise. At what points is the psychoanalytical interpretation in general and this one in particular, most and least credible?*

Wilson: A Study in Personality

The attempt to probe the motives of any human being, and most particularly of a great historical figure, is bound to be a complex and controversial undertaking. It is our thesis that underlying Wilson's quest for political power and his manner of exercising it was the compelling need to counter the crushing feelings of inadequacy which had been branded into his spirit as a child.

Had he as a boy felt unimportant? Then anything he or anyone else could do to convince him that he was uniquely qualified to accomplish great things—perhaps even something immortal—would be a balm. Had his father ridiculed his intellectual capacities and made him feel mediocre? Then anything he or anyone else could do to help him feel that he had superior ability and infallible judgment in matters in which he chose to exercise leadership would relieve him—temporarily. Had he grown up in a stern Calvinist atmosphere, subjected to disquisitions on the natural immorality of man in general and his own immorality in particular? Then he must convince himself always of his superior virtue. Had he, as a child, been overwhelmed by feelings of helplessness

* Reprinted from Alexander L. George and Juliette L. George, *Woodrow Wilson and Colonel House: A Personality Study*, published by the John Day Company, Inc., 1956, pp. 114–120, 270–273. Paperback edition published by Dover Publications, Inc., 1964. Reprinted by permission of the authors.

and weakness in relation to the masterful adults about him? Then, as a man, he must impose his will on others and never permit himself to be subjugated.

His interest in power, in political leadership, was based, we submit, on the need to compensate for damaged self-esteem. The urgent inner need constantly to struggle against these mischievous self-depreciating legacies from his early years crippled his capacity to react objectively to matters at hand.

The suggestion that such early formative experiences influenced Wilson's choice of career and his functioning in public life will appear more credible to some readers than to others. We are hopeful, of course, that the detailed interpretation of his career in these terms will be persuasive. In any case, however, we freely acknowledge that the following account is interpretative in character. . . .

All through his career his most pressing commitment, not by choice but of inner necessity, was to prove to himself that he was, after all, an adequate and virtuous human being. He waged this private battle on fields furnished by his public life. He would become emotionally committed to certain measures the fate of which became in his eyes a test of his personal worth. With his self-esteem at stake, the struggle for the realization of such measures monopolized his energy and seemed to him of transcendent importance. . . .

Naturally, there were gradations in the intensity of his commitment to various goals. Some—for example, the preparedness legislation which he sponsored in the winter of 1915–16—were purely instrumental. They engaged him personally far less than certain domestic reforms and the League of Nations, which represented the quintessence of that high and noble achievement to which he aspired with all his being. There were, accordingly, also variations in the amount of anxiety which challenges to different types of goals evoked in him. Where his personal involvement was smallest he could most skillfully respond to the demands of the situation. Where, however, he had harnessed an issue to the task of bolstering his self-esteem he involuntarily responded, in his reactions to what other people did, to his need for protecting his self-esteem. Sometimes, as in his battle with Dean West[1] at Princeton and later with Senator Lodge, he attempted to master his anxiety through unyielding insistence on breaking the opposition. On the other hand, sometimes, as when he was seeking office, he was best able to satisfy his inner requirements by highly expedient behavior.

In an overall appraisal of Wilson's characteristics as a leader, it is necessary to distinguish Wilson the power-seeker from Wilson the power-holder. Once he had rationalized his desire for office in terms of unselfish service to others, Wilson the power-seeker was free to devote every ounce of his intelligence and energy to waging a realistic campaign to attain his goal. For the personal gratifications he sought—to dominate, to do immortal work, to demonstrate his ability and virtue—could be achieved only if he first obtained a specific position of power. If, in order to gain this position, it was necessary temporarily to suppress certain behavior and to engage in practical politicking, Wilson was equal to the self-discipline required. He could confer. He could be

[1] Wilson, as President of Princeton, had quarreled with Andrew West, Dean of the Graduate School, over the location and control of the graduate college.—*Ed.*

socially charming with possible opponents in the New Jersey legislature of 1911. He need not be openly domineering. He could refrain from becoming involved in a fight to the finish with the hostile New Jersey legislature of 1912. However, having attained an opportunity for exercise of power, first as President of Princeton and finally as President of the United States, he was no longer able to suppress his inner impulses toward aggressive leadership.

Wilson recoiled from recognizing that the motive behind his urge for leadership was highly personal; that wielding power in certain ways and seeking great accomplishment were devices for enhancing his self-esteem. His stern Calvinist conscience forbade an unabashed pursuit or use of power for personal gratification. He could express his desire for power only insofar as he convincingly rationalized it in terms of altruistic service, and fused it with laudable social objectives. For the belief that the naked quest for power is wicked whereas a life devoted to unselfish service to the community is supremely virtuous was of central importance in the cultural heritage which was so bindingly transmitted to him. To convince himself of the reality of his selfless motivation, he must painstakingly carve out a sphere of competence, within which he must perform good works. He seemed especially drawn to projects which he could conceive in terms of liberating human beings from their masters—a goal sanctioned culturally and perhaps peculiarly appealing to one who had never himself cast off the yoke of parental domination. The story of his youth . . . is a saga of conscientious preparation for service. He seems to have experienced the achievement of competence and the adoption of worthy

goals as moral sanction to exercise strong, even dogmatic leadership.

Within the sphere of competence he thus carved out for himself, he felt free boldly—almost defiantly—to assert a sense of intellectual superiority. One of his friends, Mrs. Edith G. Reid, in her book about Wilson, cites a letter he wrote at the age of thirty to a former classmate:

"Hiram, I have—as I hope you have not discovered, but as you doubtless have—an intellectual self-confidence, possibly out of all proportion to my intellectual strength, which has made me feel that in matters in which I have qualified myself to speak I could never be any man's follower. . . ."

Mrs. Reid comments: "Such confidence in himself might at this time seem merely youth's bravado, but it was part of the essence of his nature—the quality which made people so often exclaim, 'Do you never think yourself wrong?' And the answer would always be the same. 'Not in matters where I have qualified myself to speak.' "

Having legitimized his drive to exercise power by laborious self-preparation and by adopting worthy goals, Wilson felt free to indulge his wish to force others into immediate and complete compliance with his demands. He could even boast about his "fighting blood" and the joy of giving it scope. The extraordinary energy with which he applied himself to the task of making his will prevail was supplied, we suggest, by the pent-up aggressive impulses which could find expression at last through his leadership tactics.

This demand, so uncontrollably pressed, for unqualified submission to his leadership lay at the root of the most serious crises of his career. It also, however, made his initial impact upon the legislative groups with which he successively dealt all but irresistible. It gave him the capacity to stand firm in the face of obstacles that would have confounded a less deeply motivated man. He was tireless in the pursuit of his goals. He was boldly inventive and skillful in devising techniques for creating support, for bringing the wavering to his side, for holding his ranks firm.

In each of the major executive posts he occupied during his life there was an initial period during which the type of leadership he exercised in response to his inner needs coincided with the type of leadership the external situation required for impressive accomplishment. He drove the faculty and trustees at Princeton to accomplish an unprecedented series of reforms. The New Jersey legislature of 1911 was a triumph of productivity in his hands. Later, he was to exact a brilliant performance from the Sixty-Third Congress of the United States.

His political objectives were shrewdly chosen. He was a keen estimator of broad trends of opinion. "... No reform may succeed for which the major thought of the nation is not prepared," he once said. "The legislative leader must perceive the direction of the nation's permanent forces and must feel the speed of their operation. There is initiative here, but not novelty. ..." In selecting the projects by means of which to satisfy his ambitions for idealistic achievement, Wilson was a hardheaded realist. They were always practicable possibilities likely to attract widespread public support and capable of realization within a reasonable time. It was the core of the man's genius to be able to choose his issues wisely and to crystallize public opinion in favor of them.

Wilson's difficulties arose when he encountered opposition, often evoked partly in reaction to his own driving demands, and when the chance for further success hinged upon his ability to alter his tactics. The trouble was that, no matter what the external situation, Wilson's inner anxieties remained the same and dictated rigid, even if self-defeating, adherence to his mode of operation. Indeed, he was usually least capable of flexible responses in the situations which most required them. For angry opposition only intensified his anxieties and the more surely dictated a stubborn determination to subjugate his foes. ...

One of the most disastrous consequences of Wilson's personal insecurity was his inability to consult about matters which had become emotionally charged for him except with those upon whose ultimate approval he could count, or with those who, in the last analysis, were not in a position to exert pressure upon him to adopt their views.

Wilson might indeed confer with key legislative leaders—although his willingness to do even that faded if he anticipated a refusal on their part to do his bidding—but such conferences were more in the nature of collecting information and obtaining commitments of support than an effort to explore other viewpoints and accommodate his own to them.

Wilson once wrote, in one of his scholarly studies of government: "... Without a voice in the conclusion there is no consultation. Argument and an unobstructed interchange of views upon a ground of absolute equality are essential parts of the substance of genuine consultation." This is precisely the sense in which he himself did not truly consult. He was loath to give anyone title to a "voice in the conclusion."

Once Wilson had emerged with a decision on an issue, particularly one which mobilized his aspirations for high achievement, his mind snapped shut. In such cases he felt that his decision was the only possible one morally as well as intellectually. Having conscientiously put himself through a laborious examination of relevant facts, he categorically identified his view with righteousness and would not permit himself or anyone else to question it. His intense religious faith—the conviction that his decisions were guided by God—served to render him impervious to criticism. A dogmatic insistence upon a particular viewpoint frequently followed a protracted period of indecision on the question. Once he had evolved his own position, he was impatient of any delay on the part of others, even those who might still be committed to ideas which he himself only shortly before had held with equal tenacity. He seemed determined to deny the complex interests which lay back of public issues, shadings of viewpoints and the bases of them. For Wilson there were only right and wrong, black and white: and he undertook to judge on which end of the spectrum various positions belonged. . . .

* * *

Whatever complex combination of personal, partisan and patriotic motives animated Lodge, certain it is that as soon as the Germans sued for peace in October, 1918, he turned all the resources of a cunning mind to the task of publicly embarrassing Wilson at every turn. He who had once proclaimed that where questions of foreign policy were concerned his politics always stopped at the water's edge, attempted, via Henry White, to furnish Allied diplomats at the Peace Conference a memorandum suggesting that the President's ideas misrepresented the real sentiments of the people and Senate of the United States. His purpose, he stated frankly, was to strengthen the hands of these foreign diplomats in their dealings with Wilson. Lodge organized the Round Robin, which struck Wilson's prestige a mighty blow at just the moment the President needed all his authority to induce the Allies to moderate some of their demands. At the height of the Italian crisis, while Wilson was standing foursquare against the Italian claim to Fiume, Lodge issued a statement to the Italians of Boston upholding the Italian position. The Shantung settlement, the justice of which was indeed debatable, provided Lodge and his cohorts with a splendid excuse to heap further abuse upon their favorite villain.

As the *George Washington* bearing the President home from the Peace Conference coursed toward American shores, Senator Lodge was deep in plans to bring to his knees the man he hated more, he once confessed, than he had ever expected to hate anyone in politics, the man whom, James Buchanan perhaps excepted, he judged to be the worst President in the nation's history. The great alarm which he and his friends were spreading the length and breadth of the land was that Wilson's League was fraught with dire danger for the United States and that the Senate must now change the Covenant to make it safe.

Almost any man who was confronted with opponents as intelligent and resourceful as Lodge and his cohorts would be distressed and angered. A more detached leader than Wilson, however, might have been capable of dispassionately countering Lodge's tactical maneuvers and of taking practical steps to moblize all possible Senate support for the Treaty. Wilson's particular anxieties rendered him incapable of meeting Lodge's challenge with such equanimity. Because he was so peculiarly vulnerable to them, Lodge's barbs affected him as the proverbial red flag affects the proverbial bull.

Wilson had deep-seated doubts, which originated in his early years, of his intellectual competence, his moral worth and his strength. He had tried to overcome these self-doubts by rigorous training and ceaseless self-vindicating demonstrations through accomplishment that he was indeed of superior intelligence, of good and "unselfish" character, and of sufficient strength to escape the degradation of capitulating to anybody. With an unerring sense of where his adversary's weak points lay and with an air of patronizing superiority, Lodge peppered him with just those personal attacks which intensified Wilson's inner anxieties.

Did Wilson, after suffering much mortification for his "slowness" as a child, joyfully discover in his adolescence that he "had a mind" and thereafter take especial pride in his intellectual attainments? Lodge was not at pains to conceal his contempt for Wilson's "mind." In a Senate speech on February 28, 1919, . . . Lodge had derided Wilson as one whose intellect and position in the world he found something less than overpowering. As for being the "scholar in politics"—until Wilson's star eclipsed his own, Lodge had enjoyed that popular appellation—why, Wilson was no scholar at all, Lodge maintained. (As evidence of this, in a book he subsequently wrote, the learned Senator cited the fact that in making a classical allusion, Wilson had once confused Hercules with Antaeus, a blunder which Lodge considered "incredible.")

Did Wilson, trained by a father obsessed with the importance of proper use of the English language, take great pains with his style and inordinately value mellifluous phrases and graceful expression? "As an English production," Lodge once remarked of the Covenant, "it does not rank high. It might get by at Princeton but certainly not at Harvard."

Did Wilson secretly fear his "selfish" motives in exercising leadership and continually proclaim his own disinterestedness and, by extension, the disinterestedness of the nation in dealing with other nations? Lodge thought Wilson self-seeking, unprincipled, egotistical, timid, narrow-minded, a demagogue interested exclusively in his own aggrandizement—and he made no secret of his opinion.

Did Wilson, desperately eager to undercut Lodge's position, make the most painful compromises during the latter half of the Peace Conference in order to obtain amendments to the Covenant which would meet the major objections which had been raised against it? Lodge, so far from being nonplussed by Wilson's coup, summarily dismissed the revisions as worthless and served notice that the Senate would have to make further changes. Unless the President accepted these changes, he warned repeatedly, the Treaty would be defeated.

Not only was the substance of Lodge's thrusts unbearable to Wilson: the Senator's manner stung him to the quick. Even one of Lodge's lifelong friends, William Lawrence, in summing up Lodge's career regretfully noted that

"Cabot" had "a certain quality of voice in making his brightest and most penetrating remarks" which could mortally offend. "His thrusts of sarcasm, his occasional sharp wit, with his manner and voice, sometimes more than counteracted the matter and sentiment of an otherwise fine and lofty speech."

As a Harvard undergraduate, Lodge had participated with such deadly effect in a traditional parody of the foibles of various members of his class that a number of his classmates were alienated for life and the tradition was abandoned. Over half a century later, recalling Lodge's manner as he lampooned his fellows, a witness of the performance declared: "I can still hear today the exultant voice of the orator. The savageness . . . repelled me utterly."

Lodge trained all this capacity for sneering sarcasm against Wilson. There was something contemptuous in the very calmness of the man: it was as though he felt the objects of his scorn unworthy even of his enmity.

Once before, long ago, Wilson had had to endure barbed criticism. Once before, long ago, he had been sent in humiliation to revise and re-revise some carefully wrought composition. And long ago, overwhelmed by his masterful father, he had submitted to sarcastically made demands and to aspersions on his moral and intellectual worth. He had submitted in seeming docility. Perhaps the rage that he had suppressed then emerged in full force against those he encountered in later years who re-awakened the disagreeable sensations of half a century and more before.

Wilson's emotional commitment to the League was . . . of surpassing intensity. Even in connection with projects of far less personal significance to him, he habitually experienced any interference in his exercise of power as an intolerable threat. Small wonder, given the very real menace Lodge presented both to the League and to Wilson's inner equilibrium, that the mere mention of the Senator's name caused Wilson to clench his teeth in rage.

If Wilson had only remained physically sound, everything would have turned out for the better. So, in effect, writes PERRY LAUKHUFF (1906–   ), formerly an instructor of government at Sweet Briar College, an officer in the diplomatic service for twenty years, and now a member of the board of directors of the Woodrow Wilson Foundation. Laukhuff reverses the cause and effect relationship suggested by the Georges. It was not, he states, a personality weakness that caused Wilson to collapse; it was the physical collapse that made him "emotionally unable" to lead. This subject is briefly discussed in other selections. The comments of Stromberg and Link are particularly worth noting.*

▶ # The Price of Wilson's Illness

Was the physical breakdown of Woodrow Wilson responsible for the failure of the United States to join the League of Nations? The bitter fight over the League in 1919–1920 is only thirty-odd years behind us, near enough to be remembered by many. It is, to put it contrariwise, already thirty-odd years away, far enough for most of the documents to have come to light and for the calm examination of historians to have been brought to bear. Yet the question remains: Why did the United States reject the League of Nations, Wilson's handiwork? Would our action have been otherwise if the President had not been physically ill? Explanation, speculation, and indeed controversy are still excited by this intriguing question.

In the one hundredth anniversary year of Wilson's birth, we may well take a fresh look at this problem. It is appropriate to examine it in the light of a great man's theory and practice of leadership, in the light of his earlier matchless successes. In so doing, we are bound to be struck by the disastrous effects of Wilson's illness on his leadership in the League struggle, one of the few instances in our history in which the capacity of a President to act has been seriously affected for a sustained period of time.

Moreover, it is surely not amiss, in 1956, to seek all the light which the Wilson experience can shed on the problems and perils of Presidential disability, or as the Constitution puts it the

---

* From Perry Laukhuff, "The Price of Woodrow Wilson's Illness," *The Virginia Quarterly Review*, XXXII (Autumn, 1956), pp. 598–610.

President's "inability to discharge the powers and duties" of his office. How costly is Presidential "inability"?

One of the great mark of the Wilson Administration was its leadership of the country in thought, in ideals, in legislation, in action. When Woodrow Wilson went out of office, a lonely, spurned, and tragic figure, he took with him a record for Presidential leadership perhaps unequaled in our history. This may sound strange after the years of strong Presidential leadership which most of us have lived through under Roosevelt and Truman. But in 1912 the tradition was quite different and no one knew this better than Woodrow Wilson. . . .

It is doubtful if any other President, except Jefferson and Madison, came to office with such a background of thought and expression about men and the leadership of their affairs. It is also doubtful if any President more brilliantly acted upon his own ideas.

Wilson's own remarkable leadership was expressed in various ways but first and foremost he leaned upon that "gift of eloquence" of which he had written, upon the art of persuasion. That he was clear, convincing, and charming to the point of magnetism, both in public exposition and in private discussion, cannot be gainsaid. Testimony to this effect runs like a leit motif through virtually every account of him. . . .

Raymond Fosdick has recently spoken of Wilson's "amazing extemporaneous eloquence," but says that it was in his informal contacts that he made his deepest impressions. "His argument was presented with a convincing skill and an intellectual brilliance." Fosdick recalls one occasion when he felt he must refuse Wilson's request that he take a certain office, and says, "With a heavy heart I went to the White House. I knew from long experience how irresistibly persuasive he could be." Wilson could move a huge audience to tears, as he did in his last great plea for the League of Nations, at Pueblo, Colorado, the evening before he was grievously stricken in September, 1919. He could likewise capture the most bitter and cantankerous opponent as he did in meetings at the White House with Senator James Reed, during the fight over the currency reform bill in 1913. Carter Glass relates that "in two frank talks he seemed to have won over the refractory Missourian, who thereafter went along with his party associates and was among those who made effective answer to Senator Root's alarming speech [against the currency reform measure]." Anyone who could win vinegary Jim Reed of Missouri possessed the *ne plus ultra* in persuasiveness!

The example of President Wilson's leadership on the currency reform is illuminating. It gives the true measure of the man, and throws light on what happened in the League fight six years later. Currency reform was a problem on which Wilson had been thinking and speaking for some years. The Democratic platform of 1912 demanded reform. The new President made up his mind he would bring it about, in the face of the warning fact that all the efforts of previous administrations and previous Congresses had come to naught. . . .

Wilson gave unprecedented leadership in this, one of the hardest fought battles in the history of domestic legislation. It is an example of the successful manner in which he exhibited the skills of leadership for six of the eight years of his Presidency, and to special perfection in the first two fabulous years.

Constructive measure after constructive measure came into being: the Underwood Tariff Act, the first general downward revision in fifty-six years; the currency reform which gave us the Federal Reserve System, that gyroscope of our financial economy; the Clayton Anti-Trust Act; the Federal Trade Commission Act, and many others. Then by his speeches of early 1916, Wilson carried the country into the military preparedness against which all its traditions disposed it. He made vocal the resolution of a united country in his stirring War Message. For a bleeding and exhausted world he formulated the great issues of war and peace as Churchill was to do some twenty years later. He faced down and won over a Peace Conference many of whose leaders were vengeful and ambitious, by persuasion and tenacity on fundamentals and by withdrawals on non-essentials. In 1919 he could stand at the pinnacle of his leadership and feel that the keystone of a new world order was ready to be fitted into its place.

At this point, the leadership of Woodrow Wilson faltered and failed. He laid the Treaty of Versailles, embodying the Covenant of the League of Nations, before the Senate for consent. This was on July 10, 1919. The ensuing struggle lasted until March [19], 1920, when for the second and last time an adverse or insufficient vote ended all prospects of ratification. . . .

Historians of the most eminent have debated the causes of this staggering set-back for the last thirty-six years. They have advanced many arguments to account for it: Wilson was too inflexible, he had lost touch with public opinion and political reality, he was a visionary, he was ahead of his time, he was consumed by hatred of Lodge, he was suffering from an advanced case of megalomania, he had sundered his ties with his moderate advisers such as Colonel House, he had lost all sense of proportion and was intent only on highballing down the line of his famous one-track mind. Some of these explanations have elements of truth in them.

Every explanation, however, goes straight back to one stark, inescapable fact. Woodrow Wilson was a sick man, indeed a disabled man, at the height of the fight over the League of Nations.

The story of those fateful months following his collapse on September 26, 1919, and his paralyzing stroke on October 2 may never be uncovered fully and accurately. For many weeks, indeed for some months, President Wilson was secluded from all contact with associates, subordinates, legislators, political leaders, press and public. Only four or five people had access to him: his wife, his physician (Admiral Grayson), and his three daughters, especially the eldest, Margaret Wilson.

There is no escaping the fact that even his Secretary, Joseph Tumulty (the Sherman Adams of those less complex White House days), was denied all contact with his chief for several months. Tumulty, devoted and indefatigable, has mentioned in his memoirs that Wilson was almost daily wheeled along the portico to Tumulty's office window where he could get the latest account of things. Tumulty was too transparently honest for his veracity in this matter to be questioned, but his vagueness is sometimes greater and his sense of dates rather less perfect than might be desired. He may indeed have seen Wilson briefly on occasion in the later winter months. His biographer, writing on the basis of carefully amassed documents, makes it clear that Tumulty did not see Wilson at all for a long period, and after that only briefly and erratically—and always under the watchful eye of that determined and anti-Tumulty guardian, Mrs. Wilson.

Through all the months of the League fight, then, who gave Wilson such facts as he was given? What was the source of those facts? Who shaped the President's thinking? Who drafted his letters, his memoranda, his messages and state papers, few in number as they were? We do know, of course, that Tumulty, working with various Cabinet members, prepared many documents on other subjects, for example the message to Congress of December, 1919, and the Jackson Day dinner message the following month (with a final editing from Mrs. Wilson). The Government did not cease to function, although it was less well organized for pilotless operation then than it is now. But it had no leader. On matters of such critical importance as the League fight, no one dared to step in.

Tumulty throws little light on the problem of Wilson's actions in this area because he could not. Grayson never spoke and his papers have not been seen. Margaret Wilson left no known record, nor did her sister, Mrs. Sayre, while the third daughter, Mrs. McAdoo, ends her memoirs with the death of her mother in 1914. The second Mrs. Wilson chose to reveal little in her book, "My Memoir." The answers, therefore, may always remain largely obscured, though there is every reason to suppose that the wife who guarded the President with single-minded zeal and kept a nation out of the sickroom played the part of regent, honestly and faithfully, as her lights allowed. It should be said in all fairness, in passing, that Mrs. Wilson had been the confidante of

virtually all of her husband's thoughts and decisions of state. She knew his mind and she knew the problems.

One thing nevertheless emerges with crystal clarity, regardless of the lack of conclusive answers to the questions posed above. From September 26, 1919, to the end of the Senate debate on the Treaty in the following March, and indeed to the end of his life, Wilson was never in a position to exert that leadership which he had so thoroughly understood and so strikingly practiced throughout his Presidency, that leadership which the Constitution, moreover, gave to him and to him alone. The failure, then, was a failure of leadership.

Just before his illness, the President had been engaged in a typical and vast exercise of mass persuasion. He had gone to the country by means of thirty set speeches and scores of informal talks in the short space of twenty-two days. His purpose was to persuade the people that the League of Nations as outlined in the Covenant was their great hope and their great responsibility. Opinions differ as to the effectiveness of this supreme effort of eloquence. The one sure fact is that it was cut off abruptly by his collapse and stroke, and never again was Wilson able to resort to this so effective technique of leadership.

Perhaps even more disastrous, he was totally deprived of the instrument which he had used so superbly in the currency reform fight—personal consultation and discussion, persuasion and conciliation with individual Senators, with committees and delegations, with Cabinet members, and with trusted advisors. The Vice President did not see him. His Cabinet members did not see him (no Cabinet meeting with the President took place from August 19, 1919, to April 11, 1920). His Secretary did not see him. Members of Congress did not see him, with rare exceptions which only emphasized his inability to use the technique of consultation to give leadership in the League fight. Senator Hitchcock, who led the Democratic forces in the Senate, had two brief interviews with the invalid President. And the "smelling committee," as Wilson called it, headed by Senator Albert B. Fall, called briefly to see if the President were really *compos mentis*. (Senator Fall unctuously said, in leaving, "I am praying for you, Mr. President." In telling this story many months later to Secretary of the Treasury Houston, Wilson exploded, "Why did he want to put me in bad with the Almighty? He must have known that God would take the opposite view from him on any subject!") There were a few others admitted for brief moments by Mrs. Wilson—the young Prince of Wales got in, but not Lord Grey, the British Ambassador.

It remains true that for the most part such communication as was had with the First Magistrate of the United States in those fateful six months went through Mrs. Wilson. This was true of oral and written messages, both. Tumulty, Hitchcock, House, and others bucked the wall of silence with repeated suggestions for an accommodation on non-essentials with the moderate reservationists, a compromise sufficient to bring together the pro-League majority. How much of what they advised reached the ears of the sick President? Who composed the replies, when any were vouchsafed?

The President was also deprived of any adequate means of sensing the currents of political and public opinion. The well-nigh intuitive ability which Wilson normally displayed to read the public mind, to sense the psychological moment for attack or for compromise, had always been a major factor in his leadership. Now he saw few if any news dispatches or editorials. He was cut off from the myriad observations of his gregarious contact men, such as Tumulty and House. He was isolated even from those directly concerned with the battle in the Senate. Sick, alone, depressed, and turned in upon himself, he no longer had any basis whatever for sound judgment of the situation or of the mood of the country.

In sum, it seems that we must draw the following conclusions. Woodrow Wilson had known how to lead, with brilliant results. Despite the bitterness of Lodge, despite the irreconcilability of Borah and others, despite the well-known post-war letdown, and despite the fact that a nation traditionally isolationist was being asked to join a world concert for peace, there were forces-in-being strong enough to win Wilson's last and greatest fight. They simply needed leadership, and they had no leadership. The great man who had shown what a President could really do to lead was physically and by the same token emotionally unable in this crisis to exert leadership in his accustomed way. It is fair to make the point, therefore, that the President suffered from an "inability to discharge the powers and duties" of his office.

Woodrow Wilson's physical disability deprived the country of leadership, the lack of leadership kept us out of the League of Nations, and quite possibly our absence from the League made possible the Second World War.

This is a costly bill to charge to Presidential "inability." At best, we must hope to avoid a repetition of a Presidential breakdown. At least, we have a duty to work out a Constitutional means of providing a substitute authority and leadership in the unhappy event of another instance of inability in our chosen national leader. The events of 1919–1920 reflect no discredit on Woodrow Wilson; on the contrary, they show by contrast how unique were his native abilities as a leader. The failure was not Wilson's—it was rather the nation's failure. It constitutes an experience which we cannot afford to repeat in perilous times.

Of the historians and political scientists who in the last twenty years have done basic research on the League fight, KURT WIMER (1915–   ), professor of political science at East Stroudsburg College, is one of the more charitable toward Wilson. In this and other articles, Wimer has explicated and defended certain previously neglected tactical moves of Wilson. While not unmindful of some of Wilson's mistakes, he absolves him of the charge of inflexibility toward the Senate. Many scholars have agreed with this view, but have faulted Wilson for not bending even further when it was obvious he could not win the whole loaf and must accept something less.*

Wilson's Efforts at Conciliation

The reason for failure of the United States to ratify the Treaty of Versailles may always be something of a mystery except that from time to time small bits of information appear which put the grand controversy between President Woodrow Wilson and the Senate in a somewhat different light. Many scholars have believed that the key to ratification still was in the hands of Wilson after his return from Europe in the summer of 1919. Evidence now shows that the President was far less rigid in permitting reservations to the Covenant of the League of Nations than appeared at the time. His approach to senators was flexible, not dogmatic and doctrinaire, not rigid and unbending. Contrary to the strictures of the late Lord Keynes, the grim schoolmaster was not "bam-

boozled" and in need of being "debamboozled." Prior to his appeal to the people in the autumn of that fateful year 1919 Wilson tried the time-honored method of conciliation. He made a very serious effort. . . .

Wilson foresaw that America would take leadership of the new international order. He felt that the United States, having ended its isolation two decades earlier, had reached its "majority as a world power" at a crucial turning point in the history of nations. In his opinion the question was no longer whether "to enter or not to enter the politics of the world." The only choice was "to enter it with advantage . . . as a leader, or to enter it by compulsion of circumstances." The latter course spelled calamity both for the United States and

* From Kurt Wimer, "Woodrow Wilson Tries Conciliation: An Effort That Failed," *The Historian*, XXV, No. 4 (August, 1963), pp. 419–438. Footnotes omitted.

the world. If Washington should fail to assume responsibility, he predicted another war from which America could not stay aloof and which would require even greater sacrifices than the war just ended. By contrast, the benefits from responsible membership were immense. Wilson was convinced membership would assure the United States "leadership of the world." Accordingly, he advocated—even pleaded for—prompt and wholehearted participation in the League of Nations. . . .

The President hoped to win support for the League through a program of enlightenment. He attributed a great deal of opposition to poor information or even misinformation about the purpose of the new organization. As early as February 1919—during his short visit to the United States—he had become alarmed by the "lies" opponents had spread and saw the need for "a systematic campaign . . . and instruction of public opinion as to the real facts and real purpose and character of the proposed League." Not wanting to launch such a campaign prematurely he considered it a "mistake" to answer his senatorial critics from Paris. Instead he planned a comprehensive campaign to begin shortly after his return from Europe—a debate which he expected to last throughout the summer. Nevertheless he did not want to anticipate conditions in the United States. When informing Tumulty of his intent to tour the country, he added that it was "impossible to predict [a trip] with certainty."

Upon his return Wilson began a program of education. On July 10 he told senators that his services and all the information he possessed would be at their disposal "either informally or in session." When the senators showed no sign of acting on his suggestion, the President took the initiative. Since his efforts to conciliate senators have seldom been adequately credited, the following schedule during the week after his return is instructive:

July 14: Wilson, through Senator Gilbert M. Hitchcock, extended an invitation to members of the Foreign Relations Committee to see him. The President's only stipulation was a twenty-four-hour notice before their visit.

July 15: The President announced that he would receive congressmen every morning between 10 a.m. and 12 noon without appointments. He discussed strategy with Senator Hitchcock, the leader of the administration forces in the Senate.

July 16: Wilson conferred with seven Democratic senators. He sent letters to eight Republican senators inviting them to confer with him at the White House according to a definite schedule.

July 17: Wilson held individual conferences with three Republican senators at the White House. Each conference lasted about one hour.

July 18: The President held separate conferences with four Republican senators. He paid a visit to the Capitol, where he conferred with Hitchcock for forty-five minutes.

Wilson was encouraged by his "clarifying councils" with Republican senators. He did not so much debate the Covenant but expounded it. Patiently and tactfully, he explained controversial sections, pointing out that most apprehensions were unjustified. He listened attentively to suggestions. Apprised that the treaty could not be ratified without reservations, he remarked that Democratic senators had given him the same information. He conceded the soundness of underlying ideas of most reservations but objected to their inclusion because a given phraseology was already "riveted in" the Covenant. Senators who interviewed Wilson received the impression that he would accept explanatory reservations which they hoped might lead to compromise. The President, too, was far from discouraged by his contacts with Republican senators. On July 18 he confided to Sir William Wiseman [a British official] that he would not undertake a tour unless he could not "persuade sufficient Republican Senators by his present daily conferences."

There was considerable pressure on Wilson to continue and expand his conciliatory activities. While senators publicly proclaimed their attitudes unchanged, opposition to Wilson was believed to have weakened. Moreover, Wilson's policy appeared to have had an effect on public opinion. Herman H. Kohlsaat, one of Wilson's close Republican advisers on League strategy, wrote to him on July 19 that "if I am any judge of public opinion you have won your case." The veteran Chicago journalist cautioned against the speaking tour. He pointed to Senator Reed Smoot of Utah, who despite strong pressure from his constituents favored reservations. In Kohlsaat's view Wilson "could not change Smoot's vote by going to Utah" but might influence the senator by talking to him in Washington. Kohlsaat suggested that Wilson see all Republican senators, pointing particularly to the favorable effect of such a course on public opinion. Democratic senate leaders including Hitchcock gave similar advice. Secretary of State Robert Lansing concurred. Cary T. Grayson, the President's physician, endorsed postponement of the trip for reasons of health. Other advisers doubted the wisdom of conciliating senators. Norman

H. Davis was of the opinion that senators would not accept Wilson's "offer to enlighten them on doubtful points" and cautioned that "the only thing that will change them will be pressure from the outside."

Wilson weighed the alternate courses. His preference was to have the treaty passed as submitted, but he was prepared to accept interpretative reservations attached to the treaty in a form that did not require its renegotiation. He even encouraged Thomas W. Lamont, a Republican member of the Peace Commission, to work toward a compromise on such a basis. The latter's report of July 25 was pessimistic, stating that "the situation has seemingly failed to clear up to any extent." What was Wilson to do? Lamont advised against a speaking tour which, he expected, would "be painted as a campaign against the Senate, and arouse further resentment in many of the senators." An adjustment still seemed possible especially since most senatorial reservations suggested to the President were interpretative in nature. Toward the end of July Wilson decided to postpone the trip tentatively scheduled for August 4. He continued his explanations of the Covenant on the assumption that senators would do their duty once convinced of the merits of the League. He was not willing, however, to put all his eggs in one basket. He was only prepared to postpone the trip until he had opportunity to test the possibility of an accommodation with the Senate. Putting a trial proposal before that body was not easy since the treaty was tied up in the hostile Foreign Relations Committee. Aware of a "perplexed and somewhat distressing situation," he was confident, nevertheless, that he could find ways of reaching the Senate. In short, he planned to test the possibility of an adjustment with the Senate prior to a presidential trip. . . .

Wilson continued to confer with Republican senators: He wanted to reach every senator not committed against the treaty or determined to emasculate it. Majority leader Lodge was not invited. Senator George W. Norris refused an invitation. But as Wilson talked to senators aligned with the Republican leadership—and he turned to them after exhausting the list of moderates—they proved less responsive to his explanations. Their minimum condition for ratification seemed beyond the maximum concession that Wilson was willing to make. On August 1 James E. Watson, the Republican Senate whip, told the President that he was "licked" unless he accepted the Lodge program. When Wilson countered that he would "appeal to the country," Watson replied: "It is too late. You are like a man in quicksand now and every struggle you make will only sink you the deeper." Shortly afterwards as domestic problems required presidential attention, the conferences ceased. In all, Wilson talked to about twenty Republican senators. At the very least the conferences acquainted the President and senators with each other's views as the time for crucial decisions approached.

Early in August Wilson's policy seemed to show results. A group of seven moderate Republicans prepared reservations which they hoped would become the basis for a settlement. Kellogg on August 7 introduced four compromise reservations in behalf of the group to clarify conditions of withdrawal, domestic jurisdiction, the Monroe Doctrine, and most important the obligation of the United States under Article X. It is widely overlooked that Wilson was agreeable to these reservations. In the Senate his spokesman Key

Pittman declared: "I am absolutely in favor of the substance of every reservation that the Senator [Kellogg] has put forward." The form of their incorporation was another matter. Kellogg and sponsors of the "draft of seven" advocated putting the reservations in the resolution of ratification. Wilson, believing such a procedure would renew negotiation, wanted them attached in a separate resolution which the Senate could pass contemporaneously with the resolution of ratification. . . .

The conference with the Foreign Relations Committee held at the White House on August 19 clarified Wilson's position. In an introductory statement the President explained articles of the Covenant believed to stand in the way of acceptance of the treaty by the Senate. These articles concerned the Monroe Doctrine, domestic questions, withdrawal from the League, and responsibility of the United States under Article X. In his view there was "nothing vague or doubtful" in the Covenant. Nevertheless, he declared himself ready to accept "interpretations" provided "they do not form a part of the formal ratification itself." He did not limit the scope of interpretative reservations. When, during the discussion, Senator Porter J. McCumber outlined his understanding of a reservation to the crucial Article X, the President replied: "We differ, Senator, only as to the form of the action." He elaborated by saying that such a reservation should be part of a resolution to be accepted "contemporaneously" with the treaty. Wilson feared "long delays" if reservations were part of the resolution of ratification. Such a procedure, he declared, would reopen negotiations. Other countries would advance reservations. Endless parleys might ensue, and the Covenant might be lost. He held that these uncertainties could be avoided by embodying interpretations in a separate resolution. In this form they would constitute an explanation of the position of the United States which would not have to be submitted to other signatories of the treaty for approval.

Wilson envisaged that the resolution containing interpretations would pass by a two-thirds vote; i.e., "by the same majority that is necessary to ratify the treaty." He had stated this view to the press shortly after returning from Europe and had repeated it to senators after submitting the treaty on July 10. Lodge challenged this procedure and contended that according to Senate rules and precedent amendments and reservations should be added by majority vote. Hitchcock, who had agreed with Lodge, was momentarily at a loss as to how to proceed. Yet on July 18, after conference with the President, the leader of administration forces in the Senate outlined the course clearly:

The treaty will be ratified without the dotting of an "i" or the crossing of a "t." Therefore the only question remaining to be settled is the form and phraseology of the resolution of ratification. It is, in this resolution, if at all that the reservations must be expressed. . . . The Senate's real issue lies simply in this one question—the wording of the resolution. That wording must have a two-thirds vote to pass.

The President mentioned his contemplated procedure to Republican senators during conferences and also convinced Vice President Thomas R. Marshall of its necessity. Wilson requested Newton D. Baker to draw up a draft resolution of interpretations. Baker, unimpressed by the merit of a separate resolution, speculated: "What difference does it make whether we get one piece of paper or two?"

To Wilson the embodiment of reservations in a separate resolution—still inadequately understood—was of great tactical importance. His reasons become apparent when one considers the consequence of adopting reservations through majority vote. When this procedure was about to be adopted, Democratic Senator Atlee Pomerene became alarmed lest "friends of the treaty [be put] in a situation where they will have to vote to reject the treaty or else to accept it with . . . hurtful reservations." By insisting that reservations pass by a two-thirds majority in a separate resolution, Wilson hoped to avoid such a situation. The test of the possibility of compromise would have come over the resolution embodying the reservations. Pressure for agreement would largely be on Republican reservationists since without a corollary resolution the Republican majority would either have to face killing the treaty as submitted by Wilson or accepting it in that form. By contrast, adoption of reservations by majority vote as part of the ratifying resolution would fail to give Wilson early control over reservations because Republicans had a majority in the Senate. To be sure, Wilson could prevent passage of the final treaty in the Senate —through administration Democrats— but in this event Democrats loyal to him would have to kill the treaty—or, more accurately, the unsatisfactory version of it. As early as July 10 Wilson had labelled this method as "very dangerous." Six weeks later he was still of the same opinion. He wrote to Lamont after the White House conference:

I hope now that all forces will be concentrated upon promoting the policy of keeping all reservations or interpretations out of the formal act of ratification, and embodying those that can reasonably be accepted in a separate document.

Wilson believed that the method he suggested would promote a genuine compromise and preserve clearcut issues. If no compromise were possible, the people could locate responsibility. On the other hand, by adopting reservations in the ratifying resolution through majority vote issues could be blurred, while opponents of the treaty could pose as friends.

Following his explanation to the Foreign Relations Committee, Wilson arranged to have a definite proposal put before the Senate. With White House approval Pittman on August 20 introduced four interpretative reservations, the content of which resembled those advanced by the seven mild reservationists (led by Kellogg) on August 7. The two drafts differed in the manner in which reservations were to be incorporated. Kellogg's reservations were part of the resolution of ratification, while Pittman's "understandings" were in a separate resolution in accord with Wilson's prescription. The Nevada Senator carefully explained the reasons for this procedure and suggested that his resolution be "considered as soon as possible, and passed, if possible, in advance of action of the treaty."

A test was at hand. One day after the President's public explanation of controversial treaty provisions, a proposition was before the Senate which had his approval. While awaiting senatorial reactions he wrote: "Everything is problematical . . . including my own personal plans." He added: "I can only hope."

Reaction of Republican senators was unfavorable. They were not willing to pursue the course suggested by Wilson. Lodge let it be known that Republicans had "the power to make reservations in the act of ratification" and planned "to exercise that power." Moderate Repub-

licans supported him, including the seven sponsors of the compromise draft reservations introduced by Senator Kellogg on August 7. Moreover, Lodge insisted that substantial changes be made in the Covenant. He particularly objected to the draft reservation to Article X of the group of seven. Moderates, in spite of their earlier sponsorship of interpretative reservations, now held such reservations inadequate. Henceforth, the real issue before the Senate was the extent to which reservations in the ratifying resolution would modify the Covenant. Pittman delayed action on his resolution.

In the showdown the middle-of-the-road Republicans stiffened their stand. Their position was difficult. Incorporation of reservations by majority vote gave them a balance of power. But their advantage was only tactical since ultimately the treaty with reservations had to pass by a two-thirds majority. They had to keep in mind the need for two-thirds approval of reservations they helped pass by majority. When in mid-August 1919 a test approached in the Senate, they intensified negotiation and exerted strong pressure for moderation on Democrats and Republicans. Most Democrats seemed willing to compromise on reservations. Their accommodating inclinations were reported to President Wilson, who was told that if he failed to accept reservations "a number of Democratic Senators will come out openly for reservations." Wilson let it be known that he considered as "premature" the very thought of reservations by friends of the treaty. Unimpressed by pleas for conciliation, Lodge and his followers persisted in effective reservations. Lest colleagues of mild reservationist leanings be tempted to pass inconsequential reservations, Lodge warned that "if it became apparent that a majority of the Senate favored ineffective reservations he would be forced to vote against the whole treaty." Behind the scenes the majority leader exerted counter pressure on moderate Republicans, especially through Elihu Root, to whom he wrote: "I come to you for help and you must not refuse it to me." What could the moderates do? The threats of the majority leader were real. Over one-third of the senators had pledged to reject the treaty unless substantial reservations were incorporated. By adhering to essentially interpretative reservations the moderates would have split the Republican Party without securing passage of the treaty. When the crisis came, they no longer considered interpretative reservations sufficient.

In August the Foreign Relations Committee spearheaded the anti-League and anti-Wilson campaign. In public hearings the committee encouraged testimony unfriendly to the President and damaging to his cause. Interested in exposing disagreements between Wilson and members of the Peace Commission, the Committee conspicuously invited testimony from members of the Commission who had resigned in Paris. By asking for information which the President felt he could not supply, they made Wilson appear unco-operative and obstinate. Provoked by tactics of the committee, the President demanded that its work be expedited. Hitchcock, the ranking member of the Committee, formally asked for the report of the treaty to avoid further waste of time. Wilson believed in mid-August that Lodge would act "promptly." Administration pressure perhaps shortened the period during which the Committee held the limelight. . . .

Wilson's position deteriorated in the second-half of August. Disappointed by

the Foreign Relations Committee, he could have ignored its renewed onslaught since it was not fully representative of the Senate. But reaction of the Senate itself to the Pittman resolution revealed that passage of the treaty in a form that did not require renegotiation seemed impossible. Moderate Republican Senators to whom he had explained the League at length seemed to have made his concessions a point of departure for new demands. Meanwhile during the period of his restraint, calculated to test the possibility of compromise, opponents made headway in turning the people against him and his project. The few occasions in August when he took the initiative did not go unchallenged. Lodge even charged that the President took "unfair advantage" when he advocated speedy ratification of the treaty in a message to Congress dealing with the high cost of living. Wilson insisted the issues were connected and considered supporting material supplied to him by the Cabinet as "very useful when the time comes to fire."

Toward the end of August the President became convinced that he had no choice but to appeal to the people. According to Tumulty "the tide of public opinion was setting against the League." Wilson realized that conciliation could not succeed. Sadly he wrote to Kohlsaat on August 27:

I must confess to a bit of discouragement about the way in which some of the men I have been dealing with have been acting. I have treated them with absolute frankness and as friends and co-operators but they have responded sluggishly, to say the least and seem more and more to show themselves opponents on other grounds than those avowed.

On the same day he announced he would take the issue to the people.

The struggle entered a deadly phase. The people were to be the ultimate arbiter of the conflict. Wilson felt he could regain and increase public support. He hoped to induce the people to press their obstinate senators. But his opponents had plans of their own. The irreconcilables contemplated a "publicity educational trip" as soon as the treaty was out of Committee to convince people that the League—any league—ought to be defeated. Lodge and his followers believed that opposition to a Wilsonian League was "rapidly growing." The Senator exhorted Democrats to accept reservations "promptly" lest "the entire Covenant [be] thrown out." Moderates also looked to the people. Having suffered a preliminary defeat, they hoped public opinion would compel a compromise. All groups thus counted on the people to break the deadlock. The result, as everyone knows, was the President's physical breakdown and failure of the treaty in the Senate.

The question arises: Would Wilson's chance for success have increased had he toured the country shortly after return from Europe? Such a course might have continued his initiative and maintained the momentum of his drive. Still, it is possible that the limit to what a president can do to force the hand of the Senate would only have appeared earlier. Wilson once wrote: "The Senate is not . . . immediately sensitive to [public] opinion and is apt to grow, if anything, more stiff if pressure of that kind is brought to bear upon it." It is likely that the President's chance of success had increased rather than decreased by his attempt to conciliate senators.

The extent of Wilson's effort to reach a settlement with the Senate is seldom realized. His talks with senators in July showed that a basis for compromise existed between him and *some* moderate Republicans. The limited number of conferences, however, gave early indication of the difficulty ahead. Surely Wilson, who postponed his trip to test the possibility of an adjustment, would have found time for further talks had they appeared promising. The crucial stage of negotiation was reached in mid-August, when middle-of-the-road Republicans exerted pressure for moderation on extremists of both sides. The failure of the moderate group to effectuate a compromise dashed hopes for adjustment. The crisis came on August 19 and 20. By the end of August an impasse loomed. If the President was not ready to yield, the real issue was whether senators could be induced to make concessions through public pressure—assuming Wilson could successfully apply it. And Wilson's writings reveal sadly that precedents were not promising on this point.

In this selection DENNA FRANK FLEMING (1893–   ), professor emeritus of political science at Vanderbilt University, evaluates the position of Henry Cabot Lodge. By contrasting Lodge's pre-1918 statements in favor of bipartisanship in foreign affairs and an association of nations with his actions in 1919–1920, he depicts him as guileful and irresponsible. His characterization of Lodge as the master psychologist, tirelessly studying Wilson's personality, lends support to the Georges' thesis, though Fleming is not in accord with their treatment of Wilson. In *The United States and World Organization 1920–1933* and *The United States and the World Court* Fleming describes the struggle over collective security during the interwar decades.*

Lodge the Republican Partisan

The position of Senator Lodge in the long controversy was sufficiently veiled that his close associates, and direct descendants, now disagree as to what he really sought to do. Some say he attempted to help take the United States into the League and others that he sought only to emasculate it.

Thus Mrs. Corinne Roosevelt Robinson, a sister of President Roosevelt, at a meeting of the Foreign Policy Association, in New York City, January 4, 1930, declared that as a guest in his house, she had breakfast with Senator Lodge on the day of the final vote on the League, March 19, 1920, and that "He told me that he was going to come back that afternoon with the promise of

the signing of the League (of our going into the League with reservations), and I asked him if he was sure of it. He said he was sure of a certain number of Democrats who would vote with a certain number of Republicans for the United States to go into the League with strict reservations, but to go into the League."

After the vote in the Senate, continued Mrs. Robinson, "I was at the door to meet him when he came back, and he went into his library with a very heavy brow. He said, 'Just as I expected to get my Democrats to vote with my Republicans on going into the League, a hand came out of the White House and drew back those Democrats, and

---

* From Denna Frank Fleming, *The United States and the League of Nations, 1918–1920* (New York: G. Putnam's Sons, 1932), pp. 475–487. Copyright Feb. 26, 1932 by D. F. Fleming. Reprinted by permission of Putnam's & Coward-McCann. Some footnotes omitted.

prevented our going into the League with reservations.' "

Some weeks later Mr. Henry Morgenthau, former Ambassador to Turkey, who had participated in the Foreign Policy Association discussion, published in the *New York Herald Tribune,* of March 7, 1930, a letter from Mrs. Clarence C. Williams, a daughter of Senator Lodge, which stated that she had been in close association and conference with the Senator during the struggle and that "My father hated and feared the Wilson league and his heart was really with the irreconcilables. But it was uncertain whether this league could be beaten straight out in this way, and the object of his reservations was so to emasculate the Wilson pact that if it did pass it would be valueless, and the United States would be honorably safeguarded. My father never wanted the Wilson league, and when it was finally defeated he was like a man from whom a great burden had been lifted."

Shortly thereafter, there appeared in the same newspaper a statement from Henry Cabot Lodge, a grandson of Senator Lodge, which read as follows:

The current discussion with regard to the attitude of Senator Henry Cabot Lodge at the time of the League of Nations debate has just come to my attention and in order to keep the historical record perfectly clear I should like to make a few observations. Mrs. Corinne Roosevelt Robinson is right when she says that no interpretation of Senator Lodge's attitude is necessary since he has himself stated for all time what his attitude was. As he has said, he gave the League with reservations "genuine support" and was surprised when President Wilson drew away enough Democrats to prevent its ratification on that basis. Whether he was disappointed or not is, of course, a matter of personal impression. He certainly had favored some sort of machinery for international co-operation earlier in his career and

in the last years of his life he inclined to the belief that fate had been good to the United States by keeping it out of the League altogether.

There is certainly no foundation in fact for the statement that he was "an irreconcilable at heart," although my personal feelings are such that I should be proud to think that he was. This thought, however, cannot be sustained. Mrs. Robinson, who was one of Senator Lodge's most intimate friends, deserves to be heeded when she discusses this question because, in addition to her friendship, she was staying in Senator Lodge's house in Washington in March, 1920, when the debate reached its climax and was in closer touch with actual events than almost anyone else.[1]

The record as to Senator Lodge's advocacy of a league to enforce peace is clear, as is that of his change of position soon after President Wilson espoused the same cause. It does not necessarily follow, however, that Lodge changed his mind for no other reason. It is well known that in the early part of the Wilson period Lodge successfully resisted the temptation to alter his stand when Wilson came to the same ground, and that he defended himself in words that are still memorable. In his famous "water's edge" speech of April 9, 1914, delivered during the Panama Canal Tolls debate, Lodge said:

I am not blind to the political temptations which the situation at this moment presents. I am a strong party man. I believe in government by parties and in party responsibility. I have for many years fought the battles of the Republican party, alike in days of sunshine and in days of storm and darkness. If life and strength continue, I shall to the best of my ability oppose President Wilson if he is a candidate for re-election and the party which he leads. The allurements of political advantage appeal to me as strongly as they can to any man. But when the relations of

[1] *New York Herald Tribune,* March 25, 1930.

my country with other nations are involved I cannot yield to them. My politics has always stopped at the water's edge.

Saying that this feeling had twice at least led him to oppose treaties submitted by Presidents of his own party (arbitration treaties) and to support a Democratic President in the Venezuela controversy, Lodge defined the limits of legitimate political warfare in connection with foreign affairs in terms that have never been excelled. Continuing, he said:

I voted and spoke against the toll exemption embodied in the canal act. I cannot change now merely because a Democratic President recommends the repeal of that clause which I earnestly resisted. Within our borders Mr. Wilson is the leader and chief of the Democratic party. In the presence of foreign nations he is to me simply the President of the United States. If in his high responsibility as the representative of the nation before the world he does or tries to do what I believe in my conscience to be wrong I shall resist him, no matter what his political faith may be. But if he is doing or trying to do what I conscientiously believe to be right he shall have my support without regard to party or to politics. To thwart the purposes or to discredit the policies of the official head of a political party is legitimate political warfare. To discredit or break down the President of the United States upon a question of foreign policy is quite another thing, never to be undertaken except for very grave reasons. In the one case we overthrow a party leader and political chief within the arena where the American people alone sit in judgment, in the other we break down and discredit the representative of the whole country in the great forum of the nations of the earth and paralyze his future power and usefulness in that field where he and he alone can declare and represent the policies, the honor, and the dignity of the United States. Conditions may arise where this last resort must be accepted, but it can only be justified by grim necessity.

Much had happened between 1914 and 1918. The whole course of the Great War had been run, in the midst of which President Wilson had been unexpectedly re-elected. He had then led the United States into the struggle and through it to victory. Much had transpired, too, to change the relations between the two men. The correct principles governing the attitude of Senators toward the Executive conduct of foreign affairs had not altered.

What then was the "grim necessity" which led the Senate leaders to demand suddenly that the Paris Conference propose no League of Nations? What grim necessity drove them to insist passionately that if such a project were drawn up it should be an afterthought of the Conference—by no means a part of the treaty of peace? What pressing need led Roosevelt and Lodge to hold a consultation, before the Conference had decided even to attempt the creation of a League, in which a programme of reservations was agreed upon? Did the national safety demand agreement upon the efficacious way to attack the Covenant before a word of it was penned?

What, moreover, were the "grave reasons" which led Lodge to attempt to send, by Henry White, to the President's prospective opponents in the Conference, a store of information for use against "the representative of the whole country in the great forum of the nations?"[2] The necessity must have been

2 Rabbi Stephen S. Wise, who was in Paris while President Wilson was negotiating the treaty, has described an active press campaign against the President in the Parisian press, directed from the United States. For a considerable time a series of articles by Judson C. Welliver appeared in the *Echo de Paris* and *Le Matin* arguing that any ultimate negotiations would have to be made with the Republican members of the Senate Foreign Relations Committee. The President had passed from power and was negligible. The articles, the cabling of

grave which led Lodge to father a written demand of Senators, after the first draft of the Covenant was approved by representatives of fourteen nations, that the project be suppressed. Grave need, indeed, must have impelled Lodge to telegraph all Republican Senators to express no opinion of the revised Covenant, pending conference, and to secure the assistance of the total opponents of the League for his reservation campaign.

It is true that Wilson took no outstanding Republicans with him and that he lost a close mid-term election. Did this omission and this failure constitute sober ground for a sustained effort to "paralyze his future power and usefulness in that field where he and he alone can declare and represent the policies, the honor, and the dignity of the United States," when he was striving to achieve a universal aspiration so powerful that the Senators, by their own admission, dared not attack it openly in their own country?[3]

Surely nothing less than profound alarm at the consequences of American leadership in a mutual effort of the nations to establish peace and security could have justified a long and carefully planned advance organization against a treaty, before it could be submitted to the Senate for its approval. What, in fact, led Lodge and his associates to conclude, at the close of a war in which the United States had helped to destroy the political system in all central Europe, that their country could play only a carefully restricted part in future world politics—if any? What had happened which would destroy their confidence in the ability of their country to play a part of leadership in the world?

In the address lately quoted from, Lodge had stated his pride in the limited pre-war leadership of the United States, as follows: "When the year 1909 opened, the United States occupied a higher and stronger position among the nations of the earth than at any period in our history. Never before had we possessed such an influence in international affairs, and that influence had been used beneficently and for the world's peace in two conspicuous instances—at Portsmouth and at Algeciras. . . . A world power we had been for many long years, but we had at last become a world power in the finer sense, a power whose active participation and beneficent influence were recognized and desired by other nations in those great questions which concerned the welfare and happiness of all mankind."

What had happened after 1914 to destroy Lodge's pride in his country's international leadership? Was he opposed to American intervention in the war? If so it was never suspected. No one was more stern in its prosecution than the Senator and his associates. They enjoyed it so much in fact that they opposed its cessation. Smash them back to Berlin! No soft peace!—was their cry, as the German lines and morale crumbled and the enemy appealed to President Wilson for peace. No one could have been more filled with confidence

---

which cost a good deal of money, became so bitter, both personally and politically, that Clemenceau had to order them stopped.

Mr. Welliver turned up later as press agent to Harding in the Republican campaign of 1920. *New York Evening Post*, October 20, 1920.

[3] The testimony of one of the strongest opponents of the League may be added. Dr. David J. Hill, in *The Problem of a World Court* (N. Y., 1927) wrote: "It will be recalled that when, in 1919, the Senate of the United States was invited to ratify the Treaty of Peace made in Paris and signed at Versailles, the whole country was at the moment favorable to ratification" (pp. 88–89).

in American power and resourcefulness than the group of leaders of whom George Harvey assumed the direction at this juncture.

What in truth did suddenly chill these men with fear when the President of the United States, in fulfillment of his incessant pledges, and "in his high responsibility as the representative of the nation before the world," moved to make permanent the position of the United States as "a world power in the finer sense, a power whose active participation and beneficent influence were recognized and desired by other nations in those great questions which concerned the welfare and happiness of all mankind?"

In 1914 no one had deplored the loss of such a position more than Lodge. He said with regret that the leadership of the Roosevelt era had been lost, both in the old world and the new. "Rightly or wrongly," he added, "they have come to believe that we are not to be trusted; that we make our international relations the sport of politics and treat them as if they were in no wise different from domestic legislation."

What had transpired since 1914 that made it proper for the Senate leaders to handle the greatest treaty ever laid before them much as they would treat a rivers and harbors appropriation bill? The multitude of direct amendments to the treaty failed, truly enough, to be later translated into "reservations," but they were defeated in spite of the leaders.

Few things are clearer than the determination of Lodge and his collaborators, formed before the creation of the Covenant, that it should have reservations attached to it. This resolve never gave way to the strongest pressure. "If the president adheres to his position that we must ratify it without crossing

a 't' or dotting an 'i'," wrote Lodge to White on July 2, 1919, "my best judgment is that he will fail. The treaty will be sent to him with reservations, and then it will be up to him to hold it back. I am giving a good deal of time and thought to it."[4]

To two visitors later in the same month Lodge gave a clearer idea of the situation in which the President would be when the reservations were presented to him. On July 21, 1919, the majority leader was visited by Mr. James G. McDonald, Chairman of the League of Free Nations Association, and Mr. Allen T. Burns, President of the National Conference of Social Work, in behalf of the treaty. Mr. Burns' account of the interview is as follows: "In our discussion of the treaty situation with Senator Lodge he summarized his attitude and purpose in the following manner: Taking from the shelves of the foreign relations committee room a copy of the general arbitration treaty with Great Britain negotiated by President Taft in 1911, the chairman pointed out the amendments and reservations made by the Senate. Exultingly he remarked: 'And President Taft never saw fit to return the treaty to Great Britain. We shall deal with the Versailles treaty in the same way. If President Wilson does not see fit to return it to our allies that is his responsibility.' Then with a snap of his jaw and a bang of his fist, 'That is the way to handle such treaties!'"

4 Nevins, *Henry White*, p. 455. On May 20, he wrote: "And what the final judgment of the people will be I do not know. There is no doubt the hostility to the League of Nations has grown, and if they adopt it, it will be a sorry day for the country in years to come which you and I are not likely to see" (p. 451).

If this expression represented a matured judgment, and a true prophecy, Lodge may be vindicated in the future for having sought to kill indirectly what he was not strong enough to prevent openly.

"Such treaties!" The yearning of the race for some insurance of settled international order made no more impression upon Lodge than had President Taft's constructive attempt to make arbitration something more than a name, or a method of settlement occasionally used for minor disputes.

The purpose of the reservations, moreover, that would encumber the treaty when it reached the President, could not have been more clearly stated, and, needless to say, the determination to affix them grew as popular opinion approved. "Strong and effective reservations will be put on," wrote Lodge again, on October 2, as Wilson returned to Washington from the West. "I feel very sure that there is now a decisive majority for them, not only Republicans, but some Democrats; and this is certain: if they are not put on, the treaty will be killed on the floor of the Senate."

But the likelihood that this method of execution would be necessary was already small. Reservations would be put on. As time passed the likelihood that Wilson would be able to keep them from coming up to him, by two-thirds vote of the Senate, increased, but in any event, as Lodge assured White on March 11, 1920, "the President would receive the blame for defeating the treaty."

To bring about such an astonishing reversal of positions was indeed an ambitious plan. To turn the tables on Wilson entirely, to leave him condemned for having defeated his own treaty, required strategy both bold and subtle. The risk was great but the stakes were high. If success came, not only would the one threat to the re-establishment of Republican supremacy be removed, but it would be possible to ascribe to Wilson failure as great as his achievement then

loomed. It would be possible for future historians to say, as Lodge himself later wrote in the concluding words of his book, that Wilson "was given the greatest opportunity ever given to any public man in modern times, which we may date from the Revival of Learning in Europe. Having this opportunity he tried to use it and failed. The failure necessarily equalled the opportunity in magnitude and the failure was complete and was all his own. No one could have destroyed such a vast opportunity except the man to whom it was given, and in this work of destruction unaided and alone Mr. Wilson was entirely successful. Difficult as such an achievement in the face of such an opportunity was, it does not warrant describing the man who wrought the destruction in any sense as a 'very great man.'"

To be able to lay the blame for the "destruction" of the greatest opportunity ever given to modern man upon Wilson, "unaided and alone," it was essential to gauge with great care just what Wilson himself would do. If the reservations were mild he might accept them and put them into effect; if they were too drastic, on the other hand, he might be able to rally public opinion to his side so strongly as to give him victory. If they could attack, in a sufficiently offensive manner, things which he would be sure to defend, and at the same time seem moderate to the public in aim, the proper mean would be achieved.

Hence Lodge devoted himself tirelessly to the task of anticipating, at every stage of the fight, just what Wilson's reaction would be. Lodge explains with great clearness, in that strange defense which he left behind him, how he performed this function. "As the final vote drew near," he records, "I felt convinced that it was quite possible that the treaty with the reservations would be adopted by the Senate because it was obvious to me that on this final and crucial test a majority of the Democrats would be unwilling to vote against ratification. But I also felt convinced that President Wilson would prevent the acceptance of the treaty with reservations if he possibly could. I based this opinion on *the knowledge which I had acquired as to Mr. Wilson's temperament, intentions and purposes.* I had learned from a careful study of the President's acts and utterances during those trying days—and it was as important for me to understand him as it was for his closest friends—that the key to all he did was that he thought of everything in terms of Wilson."[5]

To give a supreme demonstration of his key to Wilson's character, Lodge continues: "The most striking illustration of his absorption in himself to the exclusion of everything else was shown at the time of the last vote in the Senate on the Versailles treaty. After the vote had been taken and the treaty defeated, Senator Brandegee, an 'irreconcilable,' turned to me and said, 'We can always depend on Mr. Wilson. He never has failed us. He has used all his powers to defeat the treaty, because we would not ratify it in just the form which he desired.' I replied, 'That is quite true. Without his efforts the treaty would have been accepted by the Senate today.' "

There can be little doubt that this final vote was both a victory and a de-

feat for Lodge. The number of votes cast for the reservations, plus those of the irreconcilables who had made them possible, probably insured political victory, but the responsibility was less clearly upon Wilson, "unaided and alone," than Lodge would have liked. Knowing that he was within a few votes of sending the treaty to Wilson, and knowing that the tide flowed his way, Lodge believed that when the final die was cast he would get the two-thirds majority and place the onus squarely upon Wilson. If Wilson did accept the reservations, under these circumstances, the achievement which the League represented would do his party little good in the election. But Wilson was depended on not to accept them, in which case both his historical and political position would be more doubtful than it was now to be with his rejection of the reservations veiled in the votes of Senators.

The historical advantage thereby lost did not weigh long upon Lodge; the immediate victory was the main goal. But as a student and writer of history he was not unmindful of the future placing of responsibility for the "destruction" of the greatest opportunity of the age. He had plenty of reason to return to his home with "a very heavy brow" and with regret for the complete victory of which he had been deprived.

It is probable, too, that given the immediate victory Lodge would have been glad to escape the role of going down as one noted only for his obstructive power, even though his negative attitude toward great treaties might prove eventually to be preservative. But again the certainty of his conviction that he knew what Wilson would do forbade that hope if the President retained any real influence in the Senate. "This conviction held by me as to the

---

[5] Lodge, *The Senate and the League of Nations*, p. 212. Italics supplied.

"Lodge from his grave," wrote Mark Sullivan in 1926, "is still emitting undying hate against his rival in the shape of a book conceived as a self-justification but unable to avoid being partly an *apologia pro vita sua* and partly a last thrust of malevolence." "America and the League: Six Years After," *World's Work*, January, 1926, Vol. 51, p. 289.

governing quality of Mr. Wilson's mind and character," he reiterates, "was reached very slowly and only finally arrived at when I found myself confronted with a situation, the gravity of which in its public importance could not be exaggerated, and *when a correct analysis of Mr. Wilson's probable attitude was an element of vital moment to me* in trying to solve the intricate problem which I and those with whom I acted were compelled to face."

And on the last page of the book Lodge states once more: "As the strenuous days which were filled by the contest over the League of Nations passed by, almost every one bringing its difficulty and its crucial question, I made no mistake in my estimate of what President Wilson would do under certain conditions."

The purpose of this persistent re-emphasis was, of course, to drive home Lodge's explanation of Wilson's character, not to make clear the key to his own action and that of his associates who fought under the direction of George Harvey. But Lodge did inadvertently leave it to be explained why, if the campaign against the Covenant was waged only to protect American future safety, it should be of such moment to know exactly what Wilson would do. If the Covenant, amended as it had been, represented an attempt at world statesmanship the "destruction" of which would be of colossal consequence, it was the duty of the Senate leaders to approve it. If, on the other hand, it contained danger so grave as to justify rejection, the leaders should have either rejected it or set forth their terms without reference to what Wilson would do about them. There would be no need to study his every word and act to see what their own next move should be, or to determine confidently just

what their action would bring from him. No refinement and shading of terms would then have been necessary.

To the pursuance of a course of sincere and single minded devotion to national duty, regardless of consequences or of the stand of others, it may be objected that Lodge was the leader of the Republican Party, and that with his followers split, as completely as they could be, a shrewd policy was necessary to hold the party together. This is true. No party leader, either, ever labored harder or more successfully than did Lodge in the party crisis which confronted him. It is doubtful if any man ever performed a more difficult political feat. In skill of parliamentary maneuver, in ability to manipulate factions against each other, and to his own purpose, Lodge may never be excelled. If devoted service to party is a claim to grateful remembrance, the name of Lodge should never be omitted from any mention of party heroes.

Lodge's service to his party in 1919 and 1920 cost him much. In dashing from first one end of his line to the other, to hold back the over zealous and stimulate the reluctant, he incurred perpetually the resentment and suspicion of one faction and sometimes of all. Moves to ignore him or to unseat him were bruited repeatedly. People who wanted to charge ahead, to move cautiously and to move not at all naturally resented being drawn along at a common pace. Yet in the end Lodge made them sing essentially the same battle song. To change the figure slightly, he turned the roar of the lion down to the maximum pitch of the dove until the resultant chorus, while somewhat discordant, possessed the elements of harmony.

The difficulties of this accomplishment, and its aim, have been excellently epitomized by Senator Lodge in a letter of May 25, 1920, to Harvey, accompanying a draft of the keynote speech he expected to make at the Chicago convention, "subject to your revision." "In regard to the League," wrote Lodge, "no one knows better than you what a narrow channel I have to navigate in, with rocks on both sides. I want to condemn Wilson and all his works. That is comparatively easy, and I think I have done it. I also want to get the Convention to give a full approval of all that the Republican Senators did, drawing no distinctions between their differing opinions as to the final result. That is, I seek to make my speech, and I hope the platform, so broad that those of us who have fought the treaty for a year in the Senate can all stand upon it without any difficulty, and that we can use every argument, from Borah's down to McCumber's. I think the bulk of the Convention and the mass of the people at the present moment are in favor of the treaty with the reservations which bear my name. But I do not want to make any pledge as to the future."

Even after his success in holding the Republican Senators together one might have doubted the feasibility of "using every argument from Borah's down to McCumber's" in the campaign, for if Borah got what he wanted McCumber was bound to be disappointed, and if McCumber's beliefs were recognized Borah's position was hopeless. No platform and no action could possibly express the convictions of both. Nevertheless, . . . the miracle was performed to the extent at least that was necessary. From the standpoint of political strategy the only criticism that can be made of Lodge and his associates is that they performed their work too well. The prevailing political winds, measured with fair accuracy by most observers of the time, were so strong that a clear position for the League, with the reservations, might have been taken without serious risk of the resulting defection being decisive. The leaders did not certainly know this, however, and they meant to make sure.

They did so. But in the process they cast overboard without a qualm the reservations which they had labored so many months to "perfect," and which they had convinced the American people were necessary to safeguard their ancient liberties. The conviction having been generally established that the League might be safely entered, under the protection of the Republican reservations, these precious phrases in whose behalf the nation had been rocked for months were *spurlos versenkt* without a sign of regret from the coterie of Senators who had become the nation's rulers.

The election being won, Senator Lodge was content to state that "The people of the United States have declared that they will not accept or enter upon Mr. Wilson's League of Nations which he brought home from Paris and laid before the Senate. So far as the United States is concerned that League is dead."

JOHN A. GARRATY (1920–   ) has written widely on American history, but his most notable contributions have come in the area of biography. Several well-regarded biographies as well as a study of the function, appeal, and methodology of biography, *The Nature of Biography* (1957), entitle him to high ranking in this difficult art. He is in one sense uniquely qualified to speak on the League fight in that he is the only historian to have written biographies of both Wilson and Lodge. A distinctive feature of his biography of Lodge is its inclusion of comments by Lodge's grandson, Henry Cabot Lodge, Jr. Whenever Garraty accuses the elder Lodge of some shortcoming, Lodge, Jr., counters in a footnote. Lodge, Jr., having served as Eisenhower's ambassador to the United Nations, can claim certain unique credentials of his own.*

▶ # *Responsibility Shunned by Lodge; Rebuttal by Henry Cabot Lodge, Jr.*

This, then, was the complicated situation—a situation compounded of principles, politics, and prejudices. Lodge was perfectly aware, and freely admitted, that the mass of the people approved the league idea. He himself had no objection to the *idea*, but he believed that the creation of any workable organization would be difficult, and that the particular plan proposed was positively dangerous. His strategy, therefore, was to criticize—to point out the weaknesses of the specific proposal. He offered some constructive suggestions, but his main line was negative. He also thought that peace should be formalized as quickly as possible. Thus a league should not be considered until the issues of the war had been resolved.

To this extent Lodge was motivated and was acting on the basis of principle.

But Lodge was also a politician, and in a position of special responsibility. In 1918 he had been chosen minority leader of the Senate. In the new Congress he was almost certain to be majority leader and Chairman of the Foreign Relations Committee. A vital Presidential election was already looming on the horizon, and Republican policy toward the league question would surely influence its outcome. Yet the party contained many shades of opinion on the issue, ranging from the isolationist ideas of Senator Borah, the "original irreconcilable," to those of Senator McCumber, a confirmed internationalist. All of these ideas had to be

---

encompassed in a single program if the party were to mobilize its full strength for the battle of 1920. The memory of 1912 was as vivid in Lodge's mind as his recollection of 1884 was, and both memories taught the same lesson— party unity is essential to victory. This lesson was never far from the Senator's consciousness, and when it dictated compromise, he usually did not hesitate.

At this point politics merges with prejudice. Lodge never said as much, but the fact that the league was Wilson's league was of unquestionable significance in explaining Lodge's resistance to it.

Furthermore, Wilson was a man of strong views. Whether he was narrow-minded and stubborn or merely a persistent man with high principles is a matter of opinion, but in the league fight he was certainly prepared to disregard the opposition and force the Senate to bow to his will. When the Democratic leader of the Senate, T. S. Martin of Virginia, suggested at the time of the Round Robin that a two-thirds majority for the Covenant might be difficult to muster, Wilson said to him heatedly: "Martin! Anyone who opposes me in that, I'll crush!" Since the Republicans had control of the new Senate, this might seem no more than empty bluster, but Wilson had his foes in a terrible dilemma. No Senate action could separate the Covenant from the Versailles Treaty. Therefore, the opposition could not reject the League without also destroying the Treaty and delaying the peace which every American so desperately desired. "I shall consent to nothing," Wilson told the French Ambassador. *"The Senate must take its medicine."*

Traditionally the Senate had always been sensitive about any threat to its influence in foreign relations, and no Senator had ever been more so than Henry Cabot Lodge. One of the reasons he had opposed the Taft arbitration treaties had been their alleged violation of Senatorial control over treaties. He had fought similar agreements negotiated by Roosevelt on the same grounds. When the man he considered the supreme egotist set out to compel the Senate to accept without modification a plan Lodge considered dangerous, the Senator was ready to fight with every weapon at hand.

To disentangle the web of principle, politics, and prejudice which surrounded Lodge's actions is both impossible and unprofitable. Impossible because, even under experimental conditions, such analysis has defied the best efforts of psychologists, and unprofitable because in human motivation the whole is greater than the sum of all the parts. When he signed the Round Robin, Lodge was acting in what he considered the best interests of the United States *and* of the Republican Party. Patently he was also striking a personal blow at Wilson.

But this much can be said: To Henry Cabot Lodge the success of the Republican Party was of paramount importance.[1] "My first duty," he wrote

[1] On this point Henry Cabot Lodge, Jr., comments: "To say that Lodge considered the success of the Republican party to be 'of paramount importance' clearly infers that he put party welfare ahead of the national welfare. Actually there is no evidence for such an inference, and certainly the statement that he considered it to be his 'first duty' to 'keep the Republican party in the Senate together' is no basis therefor. Obviously his first duty as Republican leader was to keep the Senate Republicans together, just as it is always the duty of the majority leader of the Senate to keep the majority together. To argue otherwise is like saying that it is not the first duty of the driver of a car to see that all four wheels are on. There can be no responsible party government otherwise, and without responsible party government, the citizen is shorn of most of his power. Lodge is certainly not to

Beveridge in March 1919, "is to keep the Republican party in the Senate together." This task sometimes led him into strange company and peculiar situations.

In Paris, Commissioner Henry White read of the Round Robin in the newspapers. His experiences at the Peace Conference had made White an ardent supporter of the League of Nations, so the news of the Senate resolution and of the part played in it by his friend Lodge was most disquieting. He wrote the Senator a long letter at once, and then, realizing that time was important, he dispatched on March 9 a coded cable to Lodge via the State Department, asking him to state the "exact phraseology" of whatever amendments would be necessary to make the Covenant acceptable to two thirds of the Upper House. This message reached Lodge in Boston.

Lodge recognized the importance of White's effort to mediate between Wilson and the Senate, but he did not treat it in the spirit in which it was intended. Always suspicious of Wilson, he feared that the President was behind the cablegram, or at least, that he knew all about it. Lodge believed, probably erroneously, that the State Department censored all such cables. "It is as certain as anything can be," he wrote later, "that Mr. White's despatch could not possibly have reached me unless it had the approval of the President." Through Charles F. Redmond, his secretary, Lodge sent a copy of the cable to Senator Brandegee. He also telephoned Senator Knox, who was in Florida. Brandegee talked to Chandler

P. Anderson, who was about to leave for New York, and urged him to lay the matter before Elihu Root. Within the course of a week all these men, whose views ranged from the extreme anti-League position of Brandegee to the moderate stand of Root, had expressed to Lodge substantial agreement as to the answer that should be sent to White.

"In my opinion," Brandegee wrote, "the gentleman who sent the cable is being used as a catspaw." Knox telegraphed: "THERE IS A CONSTITUTIONAL WAY TO SECURE THE ADVICE OF THE SENATE. . . . MY JUDGMENT IS IT WOULD BE INEXPEDIENT TO ATTEMPT TO GUESS FOR WHITE BENEFIT WHAT WOULD BE SATISFACTORY TO THE SENATE." Root's line, arrived at in conjunction with Anderson, was based on the argument that Lodge could not speak for the whole Senate, and that should he try to do so he would be committing himself without forcing a corresponding commitment on Wilson's part. "It is a wise rule not to enter into a discussion with an unauthorized agent where you will be bound and the other principal will not," Root warned. Root also suggested an answer to White which Lodge accepted almost verbatim. On March 15 he cabled:

Have considered your cable March 9th. The President expressed no willingness to receive any communication from the Senate while that body was in session. If he now wishes to have amendments drafted, which the Senate will consent to, the natural and necessary course is to assemble the Senate in the customary way. Manifestly I can not now speak for the Senate or consult its members, nor can they consult with each other, nor can the President consult them while they are at their homes in 48 States.

It was unfortunate that White's attempt at reconciling the Senate and Wilson was a failure. Lodge's position

be criticized for considering it his duty to hold the Republican party together. Criticism, if any, should go to what he did with the power which a united Republican party in the Senate enabled him to exert. Professor Garraty, in my opinion in this paragraph, confuses means and ends."

was technically defensible, but it also showed up his most serious failing in the whole League fight. While always admitting that a league of nations was a desirable thing, he was unwilling to devote himself to positive action toward creating a workable one. He refused to assume any responsibility.[2] . . .

In the meantime the writing of the Versailles Treaty had finally been completed. Wilson returned to America, and on July 10 he presented the Treaty to the Senate, where it was referred as a matter of course to the Foreign Relations Committee. Protracted hearings followed, for despite his denials Lodge was determined to hold up action while the opponents of Wilson's plan developed their case. The tactics he displayed in the hearings make up the most discreditable portion of his role in the League fight.

The Committee's deliberations began on a note that would have been farcical had not the matter at hand been so important. Lodge proceeded to read aloud the entire text of the long and complicated treaty, a process that consumed two weeks of valuable time and edified no one.[3] At the end of this grueling ordeal he was reading to an empty committee-room; all the Senators had slipped away. . . .

The Committee also badgered Wilson with constant demands for papers and documents, while he in turn thwarted the Committee by withholding from them everything he could reasonably refuse to give. Yet then and later, Lodge insisted that there had been no unreasonable obstruction of the Committee's business. In 1924 he pointed out that only forty-five working days elapsed between the time when the treaty was presented to the group in printed form and the time it was reported to the floor of the Senate. Midway through the proceedings, on August 19, 1919, he wrote Beveridge: "There has not been one minute of artificial delay and there will not be if I can prevent it."[4] But this statement hardly stands up under examination. Only three days earlier Lodge had written Beveridge that holding up the progress of the treaty in committee was "one of our strongest weapons."

---

[2] On this point Henry Cabot Lodge, Jr., comments: "The statement that Lodge appeared to refuse to assume any responsibility for building a contrivance for developing collective security and international peace, is not borne out by the record. Not only had he himself proposed such a contrivance, as Professor Garraty correctly records, but in the League of Nations debate he proposed reservations which, had they been adopted, would have resulted in American ratification of the League of Nations Covenant and membership in the ensuing organization. If, in the Senate, he had opposed *any kind of a League*, the statement that 'he refused to assume any responsibility' would have been justified. But this is not the case. As the record shows—and Professor Garraty clearly admits—Lodge proposed the reservations which bore his name. He thereby sought to perfect the Covenant by amendment. He was a constructive critic. By no stretch of the imagination can this be construed as the attitude of a man who 'refused to assume any responsibility.' "

[3] On this point Henry Cabot Lodge, Jr., comments: "Reading aloud the entire text of a treaty or other document is not an unusual device in the Senate. It certainly has the merit of being germane. It is, moreover, perfectly proper to ask the proponents of any legislative proposition to read the text—which probably 90% of the proponents of the League at that time had not done. It is not such a heinous crime to ask people to know the actual facts about the subject they are so vehemently discussing."

[4] On this point Henry Cabot Lodge, Jr., comments: "Lodge's statement to Beveridge that there had not been 'one minute of artificial delay' is accurate because the word 'artificial' meant that no filibustering tactics had been used. In other words, the whole time of the debate had been taken up with matters that were germane to the Treaty. When a filibuster is undertaken in the Senate, on the other hand, all sorts of matters are brought up that have no relation whatever to the subject under discussion. This is a frequent Senatorial device, but no one has even suggested that Lodge had ever even contemplated it—let alone used it—although he certainly had the power to do so."

Given his belief that time was necessary to convince the people of the dangers of the Covenant, the temptation to drag out the proceedings was irresistible.

Probably the high point of the sessions was the extraordinary meeting of the Committee with Wilson at the White House on August 19. The event had the widest possibly publicity. The Committee gathered in the East Room, and stenographers took down every word spoken and hurried the record to waiting reporters, who, in turn, flashed it all over the nation. The meeting was an amiable one, and if all concerned had not already been irretrievably committed it might have been an enlightening one as well. But the inherent hostility of so many members of the Committee made this impossible. "We go there to get information," Lodge told John T. Morse. "We shall ask as to facts. We shall not inquire as to his views, because we do not care what his views are."

Wilson stood up well and maintained his temper through more than three hours of intensive grilling. Lodge himself admitted that the Senators were at times "rather sharp" in their interrogations and that the President took it all "in good part." The questions ranged over the entire treaty, but the most significant exchanges concerned Article X of the Covenant.

Wilson argued that a reservation defining Congress's rights under Article X was unnecessary, since America's obligation to act at the request of the League was moral rather than legal, and thus subject to the judgment of Congress.

When I speak of a legal obligation [*he said in reply to a question put by Senator Harding*] I mean one that specifically binds you to do a particular thing under certain sanc-

tions. . . . Now a moral obligation is of course superior to a legal obligation, and, if I may say so, has a greater binding force; only there always remains in the moral obligation the right to exercise one's judgment as to whether it is indeed incumbent upon one in those circumstances to do that thing. In every moral obligation there is an element of judgment. In a legal obligation there is no element of judgment.

The President seemed to think that this condition was peculiar to the League Covenant, but under cross-questioning he was finally forced to accept Senator Knox's statement that our duty under the Covenant would be "a legal obligation with a moral sanction." Since one of Wilson's strongest supporters, Senator Williams of Mississippi, had pointed out that "all international obligations are moral ones," Wilson's subtle distinction was without any real meaning.

Wilson would have been on better logical ground if he had attacked outright the idea that Congress should be able to overrule the League Council, but this would have been politically disastrous. Thus he attempted to gloss over what was actually the most vital issue of the whole controversy, one that the out-and-out opponents of the League were determined to make clear, and one that a man like Lodge considered so important he was prepared to see the entire treaty scrapped unless the right of Congress to interpret Article X was specifically spelled out.

In addition to claiming that a reservation to Article X was unnecessary, the President argued that any reservation would require a complete renegotiation of the treaty. This came out clearly when Senator McCumber, the mildest of the Republican critics of the League, suggested that, even if unnecessary, a reservation defining Congress's right to exercise its judgment under Article X might be justifiable if it would quiet the fears of many sincere Americans who envisioned the League forcing the United States into war against its will. Wilson answered this reasoning by saying: "We differ, Senator, only as to the form of action. I think it would be *a very serious practical mistake* to put it in the resolution of ratification; but I do hope that we are at liberty, contemporaneously with our acceptance of the treaty, to interpret our moral obligation under that article."

Yet he admitted, under pressure from Lodge, that there was "some difference of opinion among the authorities" as to whether reservations would have to be resubmitted to the other members of the League. He also confessed that he had "not had time" to look up these authorities. Wilson was clearly as unwilling to compromise or change his mind as were the Senators. . . .

After the failure of the amendments, the Senate turned its attention to the question of reservations. To the original four proposed by the Committee in its September report, a number of others were now added. Lodge felt very differently toward reservations than he had toward the amendments. Here was no mere question of "clarifying" his record. Aside from his own feelings, he thought that unless strong reservations were tacked on to the pact the entire treaty would fail of ratification. "Mild" reservations would not be enough. "What I fear," he informed Elihu Root, "is that if we do not make the reservations strong and effective . . . the whole treaty will be killed on the floor of the Senate. You may not realize how strong the feeling has grown against it. . . . I have no doubt that if I were to go over and vote against the treaty because the reservations were not satisfactory it would be killed. I want reasonable reservations but strong and efficient ones."

In brief, the so-called Lodge reservations dealt with the objections Lodge and other opponents of Wilson had been raising all through the debate.[5] Though some of them were unnecessary and others plainly motivated by political considerations, the chief purpose of most of them was to define the obligations of the United States more specifically and to make clear the right of Congress to control American performance of these duties. Thus one reservation stated that the approval of Congress must be obtained before any colonial mandate could be accepted, another placed all domestic questions outside the League and stated that only the United States could determine what was a domestic question, a third removed the Monroe Doctrine from the sphere of the League, saying that it was to be interpreted by the United States alone. The "Shantung" reservation, far less radical than the amendments, merely withheld American "assent" to the granting of that region to Japan, but did not attempt to overrule the treaty, and the issue of the six British votes was dealt with through a reservation stating that the United States would not be bound by decisions in which any nation cast more than one vote. Other minor reservations dealing with such things as the selection of American representatives to the League, reparations, and armaments were in general so phrased as to make clear the powers of Congress in these matters.

The most important reservation, of course, was that dealing with Article X. Great care had been taken in framing it. The final form was prepared by Lodge in conference with Senator Mc-

[5] See the comment of H. C. Lodge, Jr., below.

Cumber over a luncheon at 1765 Massachusetts Avenue. It read:

The United States assumes no obligation to preserve the territorial integrity or political independence of any country or to interfere in controversies between nations . . . under the provisions of Article 10 . . . unless in any particular case the Congress, which, under the Constitution, has the sole power to declare war or authorize the employment of the military or naval forces of the United States, shall by act or joint resolution so provide.

With McCumber at one end of the Republican scale and the irreconcilables at the other all willing to support this wording, Lodge had managed to keep the party united on this most crucial point.

During the first half of November these reservations were debated in the Senate and adopted one by one. The moderates, whose votes had killed the amendments, now cast their critical weight in the other direction. But the party of Wilson remained adamantly opposed to any change in the treaty. Hampered by the illness of the President, who throughout the vital fight remained isolated in his White House bed slowly recovering from the crippling stroke that had hit him after his collapse on his Western tour, the Democrats in the Senate were leaderless, planless, and confused. The Republicans, united, determined, and marshaled efficiently by Lodge, had the simple majority necessary to pass reservations. The Democrats, however, had the votes to prevent ratification with reservations under the two-thirds rule governing treaties. And Lodge was willing to kill the pact before he would accept it without reservations. Would the Democrats kill it rather than take it so modified? Only Woodrow Wilson could

make that decision, and he, guarded by his wife, doctor, and faithful secretary, remained almost totally inaccessible.

Finally, in November, he had two talks with Senator Hitchcock of Nebraska, who was leading the administration forces in the Senate. The conditions of their exchanges were trying, for Wilson was still gravely ill, and Hitchcock dared not risk exciting him with arguments. The very mention of Lodge's name necessitated the utmost delicacy, for it affected Wilson the way a matador's cape influences a bull. But Hitchcock did tell Wilson that ratification without reservations of some kind was impossible, that compromise was essential.

"Let Lodge compromise," Wilson replied.

"Well, of course, he must compromise also," said Hitchcock, "but we might well hold out the olive branch."

"Let Lodge hold out the olive branch," the President snapped, and the subject was dropped.

The strategy worked out by Hitchcock was weak, though understandable in the light of this conversation. The Democrats would vote down the treaty with the Lodge reservations, and then, moving reconsideration, get a vote on the unamended treaty or, at worst, on the treaty with certain interpretive reservations drafted by Hitchcock. Either enough Republican moderates would then vote for the pact to obtain the two-thirds majority, or the Republicans would have to go home and face their constituents with the treaty still pending. Misjudging the popular mind, Wilson and Hitchcock believed that the latter alternative would quickly lead to a compromise on Democratic terms.

But Lodge had control of a solid majority of the Senate. If the Democrats defeat the treaty with reservations "it will stay defeated," he told Sturgis Bigelow. This proved to be the case. On November 19 the final roll was called. The day before Wilson had sent a fateful note to Hitchcock, carrying instructions for the Democrats. The party, he urged, should vote against any ratification containing the Lodge reservations. "On that I cannot hesitate," his letter ran, "for in my opinion the resolution in that form does not provide for ratification, but rather for the nullification of the treaty." All "true friends" of the League of Nations should vote in the negative.

The Democrats followed orders. Joining them in opposition, the terms of Borah's agreement with Lodge now fulfilled, were the Republican irreconcilables, so the resolution of ratification was overwhelmingly defeated, 39 ayes to 55 nays.

Frantic efforts followed to secure consideration of the Hitchcock compromise, but the moderate Republicans had been angered by Wilson's letter and prevented such a move. Next another vote on the amended treaty was taken, but the lines held firm and again ratification was voted down. Convinced of his control of the situation, Lodge then allowed a ballot on the treaty without reservations. With every Republican except McCumber voting in the negative, this also failed. A solid year of speechifying and political maneuvering had produced a deadlock. The Senate adjourned *sine die*.

The fact that the treaty could not command a simple majority *with or without* the Lodge reservations is a tribute only to the stubbornness of both sides. The friends of Wilson placed the blame on Lodge. "He has misrepre-

sented the effect of the treaty industriously," Moorfield Storey charged, "and has brought this country to a position which is lamentable." Lodge in turn laid the impasse on Wilson's doorstep. "He would not consult, he would not advise, he would not consider any change of meaning or consequence. He was determined to have the treaty in every essential point exactly as he had approved it at Paris, and nothing else," the Senator wrote five years later in *The Senate and the League of Nations*. In 1919 he expressed himself most clearly in a letter to Elihu Root, who had congratulated him for his clever management of the fight, "one of the greatest examples of parliamentary leadership that I have ever known or known of":

If Wilson had not written his letter to the Democratic caucus, calling on them to kill the treaty rather than accept the reservations, the treaty would have been ratified on the 19th of November [*Lodge wrote*]. There would have been enough Democrats voting with us to have done it. It was killed by Wilson. He has been the marplot from the beginning. All the delays and all the troubles have been made by him. . . . We have worked for more than two months over those reservations and they represent an amount of labor and modification and concession that it would take me a long time to explain to you. He can have the treaty ratified at any moment if he will accept the reservations and if he declines to do so we are not in the least afraid to meet him at the polls on that issue.

Less partisan observers were inclined to spread the blame. Few Americans had worked more sincerely for the League of Nations than William Howard Taft. Rebuffed by Wilson, scoffed at by Lodge, he summed the situation up in a personal letter. Lodge and Wilson, he wrote, "exalt their personal prestige and the saving of their ugly faces above the welfare of the country and the world."*

* * *

* The following comment is by Henry Cabot Lodge, Jr.: "In response to Professor Garraty's request, the following comparison is set down between Lodge's principal views concerning the organization of peace, which were largely expressed in the Lodge reservations, and current ideas on this subject, which are largely expressed in the United Nations Charter:

"1. Lodge contended that the League of Nations Covenant should not have been tied to the Versailles Treaty because this prevented consideration of the Covenant on its merits and caused it to suffer from the Treaty's manifest and admitted imperfections.

"The United Nations Charter, on the other hand, was presented as a separate proposal and was considered and approved on its merits. There was never any serious thought given to tying it to a general peace treaty, which, of course, would have ended any hope for a United Nations organization, inasmuch as no such peace treaty has been possible at any time during the past seven years, because of the Soviet attitude.

"2. Lodge contended that the United States should determine whether a question was or was not a domestic question. The League of Nations Covenant provided that the League Council would have this great power.

"Such a provision today would be unthinkable. Article 2, paragraph 7, of the United Nations Charter says: 'Nothing contained in the present Charter shall authorize the United Nations to intervene in matters which are essentially within the domestic jurisdiction of any state or shall require the Members to submit such matters to settlement under the present Charter'—a provision which is altogether in the spirit of the Lodge reservations. The debates in the House and Senate and the expressions of American political leaders in the period following World War II, such as the Connally resolution of November 5, 1943, show clearly that, although the decision as to the *discussion* of a question in United Nations organs, other than the Security Council, is left by the United States to occasional decision by member states, no responsible body of opinion either here or abroad now suggests depriving any country of its right to determine what is or is not a domestic question insofar as *actions* are concerned. As regards the United States, action legally binding can only be taken in the Security Council, where we have the veto.

"In this case it appears that the authors of the League of Nations Covenant in their commendable zeal not to be isolationists 'jumped clear over the horse.'

"3. Lodge contended that the approval of Congress must be obtained before any colonial mandate could be accepted—not an unreasonable proposition when seen in the light of our much better subsequent experience of international affairs, which included the approval by Congress on July 18, 1947, of the Trusteeship agreement for the Pacific territory.

"4. Lodge opposed the idea of the United States having merely equality of voting with all the small nations who were members of the League.

"In the United Nations Charter, it is fundamental that equal voting as between large and small states occurs only in United Nations organs other than the Security Council whose decisions, while important because of their bearing on public opinion, are purely recommendatory. There is, of course, no equality of voting between all the 60 large and small states as regards the Security Council—which, with its 5 permanent and 6 non-permanent members and its veto, is the only organ of the United Nations which has the power to make 'action decisions' involving orders to the members for the use of force. In addition, the veto, which has been so abused by the Soviet Union, rightly makes it certain that American forces cannot be ordered into action against the will of the United States government. The proposal in the Lodge reservations that small and large states should not have equal voting on such decisions, directly involving war and peace and life and death, appears today to be a wholly reasonable clarification of an utterly vital matter.

"5. Perhaps the most difficult issue was raised by Article X, which, in President Wilson's words, was 'a very grave and solemn moral obligation' to commit the United States to preserve the territorial integrity and political independence of members of the League. To this Article the Senate added the Lodge reservation that military action taken in conformity with the Article should be by act or joint resolution of Congress. In other words, it was not contended that the United States should never seek to preserve the territorial integrity of another country. The reservation merely stated that in any particular case which might arise Congress would have to act.

"Consider the situation today. All the principal steps which have been taken since the end of World War II which relate to issues of peace and war specifically and categorically reserve the principle of national sovereignty and the principle of constitutional process. No responsible man suggests that Congress should be deprived of one of the greatest, most far-reaching and most fundamental constitutional processes, which is the power to declare war. In the Atlantic Pact specific statement is made that its provisions shall be 'carried out by the parties in accordance with their respective constitutional processes.' As far as I know, no objection was made to the insertion of these words and I do not recall any objection being made on the floor of the Senate to their being in the text. Yet—strange to relate—it was this simple insistence on that

power which caused so much disagreement in connection with Article X.

"The Atlantic Pact also clearly omits any thought that we shall guarantee the territorial integrity of any country. The concept of the Pact is that 'an attack on one is an attack on all,' which leaves it to every nation to decide how it shall react.

"Article X, on the other hand, by virtue of its stress on 'territorial integrity,' appears in effect as a commitment to send infantry to the actual 'territorial' place where an aggression has occurred instead of retaining our freedom to use either strategic aviation or naval power or an embargo or a blockade or any one of a number of other instrumentalities.

"Here are the pertinent provisions of this, the most important, Lodge reservation:

" 'the United States assumes no obligation to preserve the territorial integrity or political independence of any country, or to interfere in controversies between nations . . . under the provisions of Article X . . . unless in any particular case, the Congress, which under the Constitution, has the sole power to declare war or authorize the employment of the military and naval forces of the United States, shall by act or joint resolution so provide.'

"This language simply preserved the power of Congress—a power which is jealously guarded today, which is completely safeguarded both in the United Nations Charter and in the Atlantic Pact, and which President Wilson was unwilling categorically to express at that time. When one compares these reservations with what later experience has taught us in the struggle for collective security, it appears that Lodge, in seeking to eliminate any doubt on this point, was essentially way ahead of his time."

The following essay is the most impassioned of any in this book, and it points up the intense excitement the controversy can still generate. WILLIAM G. CARLETON (1903–   ) fervently defends Wilson against almost all the criticisms earlier writers have made. Wilson's practical moves to get the Treaty approved as well his grand design for peace receive high praise. At the same time Carleton levels a broadside at Lodge and his followers for both their partisanship and their myopic vision of world affairs. Carleton is a professor of political science at the University of Florida. He has written a detailed study of United States foreign policy since World War II, *The Revolution in American Foreign Policy.**

Wilson: Spokesman for Today and Tomorrow

All high-placed statesmen crave historical immortality. Woodrow Wilson craved it more than most. Thus far the fates have not been kind to Wilson; there is a reluctance to admit him to as great a place in history as he will have.

Congress has just gotten around to planning a national memorial for Wilson, several years after it had done this for Theodore Roosevelt and Franklin D. Roosevelt. Wilson is gradually being accepted as one of the nation's five or six greatest Presidents. However, the heroic mold of the man on the large stage of world history is still generally unrecognized.

There is a uniquely carping, hypercritical approach to Wilson. Much more than other historical figures he is being judged by personality traits, many of them distorted or even fancied. Wilson is not being measured by the yardstick used for other famous characters of history. There is a double standard at work here.

What are the common errors and misrepresentations with respect to Wilson? In what ways is he being judged more rigorously? What are the reasons for this? Why will Wilson eventually achieve giant stature in world history?

There are two criticisms of Wilson that go to the heart of his fame and place in history. One is an alleged inflexibility and intransigence, an inability to compromise. The other is that he had no real understanding of world politics, that he was a naïve idealist. Neither is true.

* From William G. Carleton, "A New Look at Woodrow Wilson," *The Virginia Quarterly Review*, XXXVII (Autumn, 1962), pp. 545–565.

If Wilson were indeed as stubborn and adamant as he is often portrayed he would have been a bungler at his work, for the practice and art of politics consist in a feeling for the possible, a sense of timing, a capacity for give-and-take compromise. In reality, Wilson's leadership of his party and the legislative accomplishments of his first term were magnificent. His performance was brilliantly characterized by the very qualities he is said to have lacked: flexibility, accommodation, a sense of timing, and a willingness to compromise. . . .

The cautious way Wilson led the country to military preparedness and to war demonstrated resiliency and a sense of timing of a high order. At the Paris Conference Wilson impressed thoughtful observers with his skill as a negotiator; many European diplomats were surprised that an "amateur" could do so well. Here the criticism is not that Wilson was without compromise but that he compromised too much.

Actually, the charge that Wilson was incapable of compromise must stand or fall on his conduct during the fight in the Senate over the ratification of the League of Nations, particularly his refusal to give the word to the Democratic Senators from the South to vote for the Treaty with the Lodge Reservations, which, it is claimed, would have assured ratification. Wilson, say the critics, murdered his own brain child. It is Wilson, and not Lodge, who has now become the villain of this high tragedy.

Now, would a Wilsonian call to the Southerners to change their position have resulted in ratification? Can we really be sure? In order to give Southerners time to readjust to a new position, the call from the White House would have had to have been made

several weeks before the final vote. During that time what would have prevented Lodge from hobbling the League with still more reservations? Would the mild reservationists, all Republicans, have prevented this? The record shows, I think, that in the final analysis the mild reservationists could always be bamboozled by Lodge in the name of party loyalty. As the fight on the League had progressed, the reservations had become more numerous and more crippling. Wilson, it seems, had come to feel that there simply was no appeasing Lodge.

During the Peace Conference, in response to the Senatorial Round Robin engineered by Lodge, Wilson had reopened the whole League question and obtained the inclusion of American "safeguards" he felt would satisfy Lodge. This had been done at great cost, for it had forced Wilson to abandon his position as a negotiator above the battles for national advantages and to become a suppliant for national concessions. This had resulted in his having to yield points in other parts of the Treaty to national-minded delegations from other countries. When Wilson returned from Paris with the completed Treaty, Lodge had "raised the ante," the Lodge Reservations requiring the consent of other signatory nations were attached to the Treaty, and these had multiplied and become more restrictive in nature as the months went by. Would not then a "final" yielding by Wilson have resulted in even stiffer reservations being added? Was not Lodge using the Reservations to effect not ratification but rejection, knowing that there was a point beyond which Wilson could not yield?

Wilson seems honestly to have believed that the Lodge Reservations emasculated the League. Those who read them for the first time will be surprised, I think, to discover how nationally self-centered they were. If taken seriously, they surely must have impaired the functioning of the League. However, Wilson was never opposed to clarifying or interpretative reservations which would not require the consent of the other signatories. Indeed, he himself wrote the Hitchcock Reservations.

Even had the League with the Lodge Reservations been ratified, how certain can we really be that this would have meant American entrance into the League? Under the Lodge Reservations, every signatory nation had to accept them before the United States could become a member. Would all the signatories have accepted every one of the fifteen Lodge Reservations? The United States had no monopoly on chauvinism, and would not other nations have interposed reservations of their own as a condition to their acceptance of the Lodge Reservations?

At Paris, Wilson had personally experienced great difficulty getting his own mild "reservations" incorporated into the Covenant. Now, at this late date, would Britain have accepted the Lodge Reservation on Irish self-determination? In all probability. Would Japan have accepted the Reservation on Shantung? This is more doubtful. Would the Latin American states have accepted the stronger Reservation on the Monroe Doctrine? This is also doubtful. Chile had already shown concern, and little Costa Rica had had the temerity to ask for a definition of the Doctrine. Would the British Dominions have accepted the Reservation calling for one vote for the British Empire or six votes for the United States? Even Lord Grey, who earlier had predicted that the signatories would accept the Lodge Reservations, found that he could not guarantee

acceptance by the Dominions, and Canada's President of the Privy Council and Acting Secretary for External Affairs, Newton W. Rowell, declared that if this Reservation were accepted by the other powers Canada would withdraw from the League.

By the spring of 1920, Wilson seems to have believed that making the League of Nations the issue in the campaign of 1920 would afford a better opportunity for American participation in an effective League than would further concessions to Lodge. To Wilson, converting the Presidential election into a solemn referendum on the League was a reality. For months, because of his illness, he had lived secluded in the White House, and the memories of his highly emotional reception in New York on his return from Paris and of the enthusiasm of the Western audiences during his last speaking trip burned vividly bright. He still believed that the American people, if given the chance, would vote for the League without emasculating reservations. Does this, then, make Wilson naïve? It is well to remember that in the spring of 1920 not even the most sanguine Republican envisaged the Republican sweep that would develop in the fall of that year.

If the strategy of Wilson in the spring of 1920 was of debatable wisdom, the motives of Lodge can no longer be open to doubt. After the landslide of 1920, which gave the Republicans the Presidency and an overwhelming majority in a Senate dominated by Lodge in foreign policy, the Treaty was never resurrected. The Lodge Reservations, representing months of gruelling legislative labor, were cavalierly jettisoned, and a separate peace was made with Germany.

What, then, becomes of the stock charge that Wilson was intolerant of opposition and incapable of bending? If the truth of this accusation must rest on Wilson's attitude during the Treaty fight, and I think it must, for he showed remarkable adaptability in other phases of his Presidency, then it must fall. The situation surrounding the Treaty fight was intricately tangled, and there is certainly as much evidence on the side of Wilson's forbearance as on the side of his obstinacy.

A far more serious charge against Wilson is that he had no realistic understanding of world politics, that he was an impractical idealist whose policies intensified rather than alleviated international problems. Now, what American statesman of the period understood world politics better than Wilson—or indeed in any way as well as he? Elihu Root, with his arid legalism? Philander Knox, with his dollar diplomacy? Theodore Roosevelt or Henry Cabot Lodge? Roosevelt and Lodge had some feel for power politics, and they understood the traditional balance of power, at least until their emotions for a dictated Allied victory got the better of their judgment; but was either of them aware of the implications for world politics of the technological revolution in war and the disintegration of the old balance of power? And were not both of them blind to a new force in world politics just then rising to a place of importance—the anti-imperialist revolutions, which even before World War I were getting under way with the Mexican Revolution and the Chinese Revolution of Sun Yat-sen?

Wilson is charged with having no understanding of the balance of power, but who among world statesmen of the twentieth century better stated the classic doctrine of the traditional balance of power than Wilson in his famous Peace Without Victory speech? And was it not

Theodore Roosevelt who derided him for stating it? With perfectly straight faces Wilson critics, and a good many historians, tell us that TR, who wanted to march to Berlin and saddle Germany with a harsh peace, and FDR, who sponsored unconditional surrender, "understood" the balance of power, but that Wilson, who fought to salvage a power balance by preserving Germany from partition, was a simple-simon in world politics—an illustration of the double standard at work in evaluating Wilson's place in history.

Wilson not only understood the old, but with amazing clarity he saw the new, elements in world politics. He recognized the emergence of the anti-imperialist revolutions and the importance of social politics in the international relations of the future. He recognized, too, the implications for future world politics of the technological revolution in war, of total war, and of the disintegration of the old balance of power—for World War I had decisively weakened the effective brakes on Japan in Asia, disrupted the Turkish Empire in the Middle East and the Austro-Hungarian Empire in Europe, and removed Russia as a make-weight for the foreseeable future. Wilson believed that a truncated Germany and an attempted French hegemony would only add to the chaos, but he saw too that merely preserving Germany as a power unit would not restore the old balance of power. To Wilson, even in its prime the traditional balance of power had worked only indifferently and collective security would have been preferable, but in his mind the revolutionary changes in the world of 1919 made a collective-security system indispensable.

Just what is realism in world politics? Is it not the ability to use purposefully many factors, even theoretically contradictory ones, and to use them not singly and consecutively but interdependently and simultaneously, shifting the emphasis as conditions change? If so, was not Wilson a very great realist in world politics? He used the old balance-of-power factors, as evidenced by his fight to save Germany as a power unit and his sponsoring of a tripartite alliance of the United States, Britain, and France to guarantee France from any German aggression until such time as collective security would become effective. But he labored to introduce into international relations the new collective-security factors to supplement and gradually supersede in importance the older factors, now increasingly outmoded by historical developments. To label as doctrinaire idealist one who envisaged world politics in so broad and flexible a way is to pervert the meaning of words. . . .

It cannot be denied that Wilson himself did much to fashion the extraordinarily high yardstick by which he has been measured. Even when Wilson saw things more clearly and realistically than his contemporaries—which he did a great part of the time—he had a way of verbalizing the situation and the goals in idealistic, even poetic, terms. When Wilson's social and political gains were great—as they often were—they sometimes fell short of the expectations he had aroused. But it must always be remembered that if he had not aroused those expectations, had not lifted men above and beyond themselves, his gains would not have been as great as in fact they were. In many of its aspects, the Treaty of Versailles failed to come up to Wilson's aims; but it founded the world's first collective-security organization and in other ways was a better peace than it would have been had not

Wilson voiced his conceptions of a just peace and fought at Paris to achieve them. However, this characteristic in Wilson to arouse expectations beyond literal fulfillment has frequently resulted in his being measured not by the ordinary standards of history but by his own loftier ones.

Finally, in the public mind all of Wilson's achievements were overshadowed by the defeat of the League, and he became synonymous with failure. Time, a further unfolding of events, and a better understanding of the problems and trends of the twentieth century were required for Wilson to emerge as the symbol of prophetic insight. . . .

In my own evaluation, I place Wilson along with Jefferson and Lincoln as the nation's three greatest Presidents, which makes Wilson - our greatest twentieth-century President. If rated solely on the basis of long-range impact on international relations, Wilson is the most influential of all our Presidents.

What are the achievements which entitle Wilson to so high a place? Let us consider the major ones, although of course some of these are more important than others.

First, as John M. Blum, one of Wilson's most perceptive biographers, observes, Wilson put together an alliance of elements which later was to be the basis of the New Deal strength. . . .

Second, the New Deal reforms were built on the Wilson reforms. . . .

Third, Wilson by 1916 had clarified reform in an intellectual way, given it a rationale which demonstrated that under the conditions of the twentieth century the extension of federal power for economic and social reform was not an impairment of traditional American liberty and democracy but an enlargement of them. . . .

Fourth, better than any responsible statesman of his day, Wilson understood and sympathized with the anti-imperialist revolutions and their aspirations for basic internal reforms. He withdrew American support for the Bankers' Consortium in China, and the United States under Wilson was the first of the great powers to recognize the Revolution of Sun Yat-sen. Early in his term he had to wrestle with the Mexican Revolution. He saw the need for social reform; avoided the general war with Mexico that many American investors, Catholics, and professional patriots wanted; and by refusing to recognize the counter-revolution of Huerta and cutting Huerta off from trade and arms while allowing the flow of arms to Carranza, Villa, and Zapata, he made possible the overthrow of the counter-revolution and the triumph of the Revolution. What merciless criticism was heaped on Wilson for insisting that Latin Americans should be positively encouraged to institute reforms and develop democratic practices. Yet today Americans applaud their government's denial of Alliance-for-Progress funds to Latin American countries which refuse to undertake fundamental economic and social reforms and flout democracy.

Fifth, confronted with the stupendous and completely novel challenge of having to mobilize not only America's military strength but also its civilian resources and energies in America's first total war, the Wilson Administration set up a huge network of administrative agencies, exemplifying the highest imagination and creativity in the art of practical administration. FDR, in his New Deal and in his World War II agencies, was to borrow heavily from the Wilson innovations.

Sixth, Wilson's Fourteen Points and his other peace aims constituted war propaganda of perhaps unparalleled brilliance. They thrilled the world. They gave high purpose to the peoples of the Allied countries and stirred their war efforts. Directed over the heads of the governments to the enemy peoples themselves, they produced unrest, helped bring about the revolutions that overthrew the Sultan, the Hapsburgs, and the Hohenzollerns, and hastened the end of the war.

Seventh, the Treaty of Versailles, of which Wilson was the chief architect, was a better peace than it would have been (considering, among other things, the imperialist secret treaties of the Allies) because of Wilson's labors for a just peace. The League of Nations was founded, and this was to be the forerunner of the United Nations. To the League was assigned the work of general disarmament. The mandate system of the League, designed to prepare colonial peoples for self-government and national independence, was a revolutionary step away from the old imperialism. The aspirations of many peoples in Europe for national independence were fulfilled. (If the disruption of the Austro-Hungarian Empire helped destroy the old balance of power, it must be said that in this particular situation Wilson's doctrine of national autonomy only exploited an existing fact in the interest of Allied victory, and even had there been no Wilsonian self-determination the nationalities of this area were already so well developed that they could not have been denied independence after the defeat of the Hapsburgs. Wilson's self-determination was to be a far more *creative* force among the colonial peoples than among the Europeans.) The Treaty restrained the chauvinism of the Italians, though not as much as Wilson would have liked. It prevented the truncating of Germany by preserving to her the Left Bank of the Rhine. The war-guilt clause and the enormous reparations saddled on Germany were mistakes, but Wilson succeeded in confining German responsibility to civilian damage and the expenses of Allied military pensions rather than the whole cost of the war; and had the United States ratified the Treaty and participated in postwar world affairs, as Wilson expected, the United States would have been in a position to join Britain in scaling down the actual reparations bill and in preventing any such adventure as the French seizure of the Ruhr in 1923, from which flowed Germany's disastrous inflation and the ugly forces of German nihilism. (There is poignancy in the broken Wilson's coming out of retirement momentarily in 1923 to denounce France for making "waste paper" of the Treaty of Versailles.) Finally, if Shantung was Wilson's Yalta, he paid the kind of price FDR paid and for precisely the same reason—the collapse of the balance of power in the immediate area involved.

Eighth, the chief claim of Wilson to a superlative place in history—and it will not be denied him merely because he was turned down by the United States Senate—is that he, more than any other, formulated and articulated the ideology which was the polestar of the Western democracies in World War I, in World War II, and in the decades of Cold War against the Communists. Today, well past the middle of the twentieth century, the long-time program of America is still a Wilsonian program: international collective security, disarmament, the lowering of economic barriers between nations (as in America's support for the developing West European community today), anti-colonialism, self-determination of nations, and democratic social politics as an alternative to Communism. And this was the program critics of Wilson called "anachronistic," a mere "throw-back" to nineteenth-century liberalism!

America today is still grappling with the same world problems Wilson grappled with in 1917, 1918, and 1919, and the programs and policies designed to meet them are still largely Wilsonian. But events since Wilson's time have made his solutions more and more prophetic and urgent. The sweep of the anti-imperialist revolutions propels us to wider self-determination and social politics. The elimination of space, the increasing interdependence of the world, the further disintegration of the balance of power in World War II, and the nuclear revolution in war compel us to more effective collective security and to arms control supervised by an agency of the United Nations. . . .

ROBERT E. OSGOOD (1921–   ) is, like Carleton, a political scientist, but there almost all resemblance ends, as far as their view of Wilson is concerned. A student of McGeorge Bundy at Harvard, where he received his Ph.D. in 1952, and now professor of American foreign policy at the Johns Hopkins School of Advanced International Studies and research associate at the Washington Center of Foreign Policy Research of Johns Hopkins University, Osgood belongs to the Realist school of writers on American foreign policy. In his doctoral dissertation, published as *Ideals and Self-Interest in America's Foreign Relations*, he analyzes the conflicts between different approaches to international politics. Like other Realists, such as Hans Morgenthau and George Kennan, he regards Woodrow Wilson's approach as having had particularly deplorable consequences. Fortunately, he feels, we have discarded much of the legalistic-moralistic tone of Wilsonianism in favor of *Realpolitik.**

Wilson's Concepts Unrealistic Today

In our foreign relations we have made a revolutionary break with the past; yet we are haunted by the ghosts of history. However dissimilar the two periods may be, we approach the problems of the cold war in the perspective of 1917–1941. The events of that momentous quarter-century destroyed America's illusion of isolation and set the stage for its present role as one of the world's two most active interventionists. Through our interpretation of these events we find some meaning and pattern—some historical continuity—in the transformation in our foreign policy. The lessons of history form a bridge between the past and the present. They help us to explain the shattering of our traditional image of the outside world, and they serve as a guide for avoiding the "mistakes" that propelled the nation into its present time of troubles.

Yet precisely because we regard the lessons of history as a bridge between our current adversities and a past with which we are reluctant to break entirely, we seek in these lessons some vindication of our present policies that will establish a bond with our traditional approach to foreign relations. We find this bond, above all, in the lesson of collective security—in the belief that we are now conducting, or should be conducting, our foreign relations according to

---

*From Robert E. Osgood, "Woodrow Wilson, Collective Security, and the Lessons of History," *Confluence*, V (Winter, 1957), pp. 341–354. Footnotes omitted.

this principle, which is said to be a true expression of America's mission in the world, but which we failed to live up to after the First World War, thereby facilitating a chain of aggression that culminated in the Second World War.

There is a moral and emotional quality about our belief in collective security that elevates it above a mere historical interpretation to the status of a primary tenet of foreign policy. It is as though we envisioned world affairs as a gigantic morality play, in which every action is part of a necessary sequence that punishes national sin and rewards national virtue with perfect justice. The United States, with the burden of history upon its shoulders, is the chief actor in this drama. Because the United States rejected the League of Nations—the story goes—it eventually paid the penalty of involvement in a terrible world war. But now—we repeatedly tell ourselves and the world—we have dedicated American policy to strengthening the system of collective security which we mistakenly rejected in our period of isolation. There is no more prominent theme in American pronouncements on foreign policy throughout the last decade than the affirmation of collective security as the guiding objective of our foreign relations. With a repetitiveness bordering upon incantation, Democratic and Republican spokesmen alike have expounded and justified America's postwar entanglements and interventions in the vocabulary of collective security, as if the god of History could be propitiated by redeeming past errors with declarations of present rectitude.

In this international morality play Woodrow Wilson is, of course, the central figure—a kind of Moses—since it was he who made collective security an

American policy, enshrined it in the Covenant of the League of Nations, and then, tragically, failed to gain America's adherence to the instrument he had fashioned. The story of Wilson's vision and the obstruction of that vision is still a poignant episode in our national memory. Today many are doubtful about the wisdom of Wilson's methods in seeking the Senate's consent to the Treaty of Versailles, which incorporated the League Covenant. Robert Sherwood has written of Franklin Roosevelt's preoccupation with avoiding Wilson's tactical errors. But the vision of collective security itself remains untarnished in the eyes of the nation as a whole. We regard our present support of the United Nations and our leadership of an anti-Communist coalition as a vindication of Wilson's vision.

No one should begrudge Americans what solace and inspiration they can derive from recanting past errors and pursuing their true historical destiny. The only trouble is that in paying this particular debt to History we are in danger of falsifying Wilson's conception of collective security and—what is much more serious—misconceiving our own.

"Collective security"—a phrase that entered into our vocabulary only after Wilson's time—can cover a wide range of phenomena, from military alliances to world government; but its significance as a tenet of American foreign policy rests upon the implication it conveys of the moral superiority of organized police action in behalf of the international community over the independent exercise of national power for purely selfish ends. Certainly it was this same moral implication that distinguished Wilson's conception of collective security. Yet a faithful interpretation of Wilson's view of an association of nations reveals how poorly his conception of collective security fits contemporary American practice and how badly the prevailing American conception of collective security is distorted by the efforts to reconcile the two.

President Wilson's conception of collective security posited a system of international organization in which all nations would recognize an obligation to combine against any nation guilty of aggression, as determined by impartial procedures and laws. This conception reflected Wilson's conviction, which emerged in the course of his own futile efforts to uphold America's neutral rights while keeping the nation out of war, that modern war had reached such dimensions that neutrality was no longer possible. Henceforth, he concluded, if peace were to be preserved, all nations would have to subordinate their special immediate interests to their common long-run interest in maintaining a system of international law and order. All nations would have to regard aggression upon one nation as aggression upon all, instead of each nation resting its security upon its independent power and the power of allies to counter only those aggressions that happened to threaten its special interests. Just as policemen are obliged to combat crime rather than particular criminals as their private interests may dictate, so sovereign nations would be obliged to oppose aggression as such, not merely particular aggressors under particular circumstances. In short, Wilson envisioned nothing less than a community of power, built upon universal obligations, as the indispensable alternative to the outmoded system of the balance of power. He envisioned a "new and more wholesome diplomacy" based upon general principles of law and justice, in place of the old-style diplomacy based upon the selfish pursuit of power politics.

Clearly, Wilson's ideal is a far cry from what we call collective security today. We share his appreciation of the necessity of concerting power in order to deter and resist aggression, and we recognize that aggression anywhere in the world is likely to affect our interests in one degree or another. But neither the United States nor any other nation in its right mind is willing to subordinate its special security interests to a hypothetical general interest in maintaining a stable international order, especially if that subordination would impose a claim upon its armed forces. The United States, like every nation, must choose the aggression it opposes and the method of opposition, according to the particular circumstances and the calculated effect of alternative courses of action upon its power position. The government may decide that a particular aggression, even though its immediate effect upon national security is slight, poses an ultimate threat to America's power position that demands an effort of resistance; but rationally it must base this decision on the criteria of *Realpolitik* rather than of international law and universal moral principles, regardless of whether the two kinds of criteria happen to coincide. For otherwise the nation would almost certainly place itself in the anomalous position of having squandered its capacity to resist aggression—even its capacity to defend its most vital interests—for the sake of maintaining a system designed to make aggression in general unprofitable.

We have attached the phrase "collective security" primarily to our policies with respect to two types of international arrangements: (a) regional alliances, such as NATO, and (b) the United Nations. But in neither case have we acted in accordance with the principle of collective security as President Wilson envisioned it.

To be sure, the North Atlantic Treaty prescribes that an attack on one member shall be regarded as an attack upon all; but its membership is confined to a group of nations sharing a common security interest, who combined to form a military alliance against a particular potential aggressor; and the obligations it imposes upon its members are narrowly defined so as to serve only that common security interest. The organization will be viable only so long as its members continue to feel the need of combining against the common threat that brought them together in the first place.

This is precisely the kind of entangling alliance, designed to promote a particular alignment of power, that President Wilson hoped would be replaced by a universal concert of nations. Repeatedly, he contrasted such balance-of-power arrangements with his conception of a community of power, which would *disentangle* nations from the kinds of combinations in which they sought only their own separate interests and based their policies on selfish advantage rather than "the general moral judgment of mankind." "If you do not have this universal concert," he declared, "you have what we have always avoided, necessary alignment of this or that nation with one other nation or with some other group of nations." He maintained that although America, true to its traditional principles, had consistently sought to avoid special alignments of power, a *concert* of nations

was the very embodiment of the American mission, because we had always sought to be the impartial mediator of justice and right. To perceive the contradiction between Wilson's conception of collective security and our own, one has but to imagine the disastrous effect which the application of universal obligations would have upon NATO: its members, instead of concentrating their armed strength for the defense of a special strategic area, would have to spread their forces throughout the world in order to be prepared to resist aggression wherever it might occur.

The United Nations Charter, like the League Covenant, purports to affirm the universal moral and legal obligations propounded in Wilson's conception of collective security. Like the Covenant, it is based on the principle that all nations have such a compelling interest in maintaining an international system for peace and order that a unilateral resort to violence against any nation constitutes an offense against all. However, in the United Nations, as in the League, collective action against aggression has not actually depended upon all nations subordinating their immediate interests to the welfare of the organization, but rather upon the few nations who possess a preponderance of world power displaying unanimous approval of, or at least common acquiescence in, measures for dealing with the situation at hand. This fact is recognized in the provisions of the Charter and Covenant, in official interpretations of them and, most conspicuously, in the practice of member-nations. Great-power unanimity or acquiescence have, in turn, depended not upon the dictates of universal legal and moral obligations, but rather upon the existence of an alignment of interests and a distribution of power such that these nations have found it to their self-interest to support, or at least not actively to resist, measures taken in the name of the international organization. Manifestly, this necessary political condition has existed only sporadically.

The fact that the preponderance of world power is currently concentrated in the hands of the United States and the Soviet Union, whose interests and aims are antagonistic, only exacerbates the fundamental political difficulties involved in attempting to put the universal obligations of an international organization into practice in a world of sovereign states. In practice, the legal and moral obligations of the United Nations have resulted in collective action to deter or resist aggression only when the configurations of power and interest among United Nations members—and especially the permanent members of the Security Council—have made it to the political advantage of enough nations and the right nations to carry out these obligations or permit others to carry them out. . . .

This is not to say that the United Nations has had no influence upon the struggle for power in the pursuit of national security. The truth is, rather, that it has added a new dimension to power politics by establishing new procedures and institutional arrangements through which the traditional struggle for power must operate. The point is simply that the kind of power politics that Wilson abhorred has not been abjured in favor of the New Diplomacy, which he expected to spring up around the universal obligations of a concert of nations. No nation is willing to subordinate its special security interests to the general requirements of a system of law designed to protect a hypothetical international community. This being the case, the decisive factor determining the effectiveness or ineffectiveness of collective security arrangements is not their legal and moral obligations, but the accompanying configurations of power and interest. If these are the decisive element, then the breakdown of international security culminating in the Second World War may properly be attributed to the failure of the United States to concert its power with the status quo nations in checking the expansion of fascist power, and not, simply, to the failure of the United States to follow Wilson's leadership in joining the League of Nations. And by the same token, the containment of the Soviet Union will depend primarily upon the way in which we manage our power and prestige in competition with the Communist bloc, rather than upon the rights and wrongs of national conduct according to the UN Charter.

Nevertheless, the conception of collective security that Wilson expounded remains a powerful influence upon our minds, since it is infinitely more compatible with our traditional image of America's role in the world than the policies we are compelled to pursue in reality. In order to retain a sense of continuity with our traditional outlook we are tempted to bring conception and reality into closer harmony by two methods, neither of which promotes our recognition of the true state of affairs: on the one hand, we read our contemporary practice of collective security into Wilson's conception; on the other hand, we read Wilson's conception of collective security into our own practice.

The first method is, perhaps, of more interest to historians than to anyone else; but in an era in which history has a pervasive influence upon policy, the interpretation of Wilson's conception of collective security is of more than academic significance. In terms of our own experience it is easy to believe that Woodrow Wilson, despite his high-flown rhetoric, made concessions to national self-interest and power politics in his mind similar to the ones we make today in practice; that he was really swayed much more by the imperatives of national security and the balance of power and much less by universal principles than he professed to be or, perhaps, than he even realized. It is hard—for the student of international relations, at least —to believe that Wilson meant what he said or knew what he meant when he propounded his conception of collective security, because his views seem so implausible in the light of our contemporary knowledge of the limited efficacy of universal principles in international politics. Certainly—we reason—he must really have understood that the concert of nations he advocated would rest upon a particular configuration of power and interests, even though he preferred to clothe this fact in the palatable generalities of internationalism.

Yet actually, Wilson's views are not at all implausible in terms of America's national experience and the assumptions about international relations then prevalent throughout the Western world. Indeed, it would have been truly implausible for Wilson to have demonstrated a political sophistication which— if one excludes the early years of independence—has only appeared in the United States on a significant scale during the past decade or two, under circumstances he could not have imagined in his relatively placid and secure age.

Wilson's conception of collective security was firmly rooted in nineteenth-century liberalism and twentieth-century progressivism. It was perfectly compatible with ideas commonly propounded by the reformers of his age. These ideas revolved about the assumption that as democratic institutions spread throughout the world and as trade and commerce drew nations together, the peoples of the world would gradually acquire a better knowledge of their naturally harmonious interests and would become increasingly willing to act in accordance with them, until eventually (and in the decade before the first World War "eventually" might mean within the same generation) all nations would observe the same standards of reasonableness and good will that existed among individuals. Wilson and the great body of international reformers of his age expected that when this stage of human progress should be reached, international society would constitute a universal legal community in which conflicts would be composed according to legal rules enforced by the enlightened opinion of mankind.

These ideas are quite explicit in Wilson's writings, in his public addresses and in his private letters. . . . From his days as a young scholar through the years of his Presidency, Wilson's whole character, the substance of his thoughts, and the nature of his actions manifest a supreme confidence in the power of moral principles to prevail over selfish and material interests. This confidence was particularly marked and its practical consequences especially significant in the sphere of international relations, where Wilson envisioned the United States fulfilling its God-given mission to establish the reign of law and bring about the standards of conduct among nations that applied among individuals. . . .

The truth is that Wilson's ideas were a product of *his* age and no other. If we appraise his conception of collective security in terms of his own representation of it, we can better appreciate the extent to which it emerged from idealistic assumptions about international relations which are incompatible with the present realities. To be sure, Wilson was not able to fashion the Versailles peace settlement into a perfect embodiment of his conception of collective security; and had he been President and the United States a member of the League, he would certainly not have been able to conduct foreign policy on the basis of the universal moral and legal principles which he would undoubtedly have continued to affirm. But it is precisely because the United States had not yet intimately experienced the sobering difficulties of reconciling power politics and international organization that Wilson could expound his conception of universal obligations with such genuine and unambiguous conviction.

Today our approach to collective security cannot help being ambiguous; for, on the one hand, we covet the symbols of universality that Wilson exalted, yet, on the other hand, we must recognize that our security depends not upon "the guarantees of a universal covenant" but upon the configurations of power in their relation to our special interests. Although we live and act in the world of power politics, we are reluctant to acknowledge a fact so contrary to our traditional image of America's international role. So we try to get the best of both worlds by talking—and to some extent thinking—in terms of Wilson's conception of collective security, while making concessions to power politics on an *ad hoc* basis. If we must also speak the language of power— "situations of strength," "military shield," "massive retaliation," etc.—this does not keep us from seizing every opportunity, especially when expediency and the obligations of the United Nations Charter coincide, to assure ourselves and the world that the determining objective of our policy is really the impartial support of universal law and justice in behalf of the international community. In this way we read Wilson's pure conception of collective security into our own corrupted practice. We envision the United States as leading the civilized world in establishing the reign of law. We see ourselves recanting the mistakes of the past and taking up the banner of peace-maker, which Wilson had so gallantly offered and we had so meanly rejected. In this image of our contemporary role there is enough truth mixed with historical myth to lend the color of a crusade to policies and actions that are repugnant on straight strategic grounds.

But one may wonder what difference it makes if we console ourselves with a myth as long as we are compelled, in practice, to conduct our policies as the realities dictate. The only answer is that our longing for the myth may inhibit our adjustment to the realities. The problems of the cold war, the problems of containment, cannot be resolved in terms of the general goals of opposing aggression and upholding collective security. They are concrete military and political problems which require the coherent management of national power according to an overall strategic plan for achieving specific security objectives. Our commitment to the ideal conception of collective security becomes a liability only when it conceals this necessary basis of action and leaves us straddled awkwardly between two worlds —the one, a world of aspirations; the other, a world of power politics— bridged only by a succession of pragmatic improvisations to meet a series of unanticipated crises. We shall be in a better position to avoid this liability when we can retain Wilson's conception as an ultimate aspiration but repay our debt to History with a candid acknowledgment that we live in a world he never envisioned.

For almost two decades ARTHUR S. LINK (1920–   ) has been engaged in writing a multivolume biography of Wilson. When completed (five volumes have appeared to date), it surely will take its place among the monumental works of historical writing. Reviewers have been virtually unanimous in praising the depth of research and balanced judgments that Link brings to his subject. Happily, Link has taken time out to write more speculatively about Wilson's later years before reaching that stage in his biography. In this excerpt from *Wilson the Diplomatist*, he gives his conclusions as of 1957. Link, in addition to his teaching duties at Princeton University, serves as Director of the Wilson Papers.*

Wilson: Statesman or Prophet?

Virtually all historians now agree that Wilson's refusal to permit his followers in the Senate to approve the treaty with the Lodge reservations was an error of tragic magnitude. Having built so grandly at Paris, having fought so magnificently at home for his creation, he then proceeded by his own hand to remove the cornerstone of his edifice of peace. Why? Were there inner demons of pride and arrogance driving him to what one historian has called "the supreme infanticide"? Did his illness and seclusion prevent him from obtaining a realistic view of the parliamentary situation, or so disarrange him emotionally that he became incompetent in the tasks of statesmanship? Or was he simply an idealist who would

make no compromises on what he thought were fundamental principles?

The historian, who sees through a glass darkly when probing the recesses of the mind, is not able to give final answers to questions like these. Wilson, for all his high-mindedness and nobility of character, was headstrong and not much given to dealing graciously or to compromising with men whom he distrusted and disliked. Once before, in a violent dispute at Princeton over control of the graduate school, he had revealed these same traits and suffered defeat because he could not work with men whom he did not trust. The sympathetic biographer would like to believe that it was his illness, which aggravated his bitterness and his sense of

* From Arthur S. Link, *Wilson the Diplomatist, A Look at His Major Foreign Policies* (Baltimore: The Johns Hopkins Press, 1957), pp. 153–156. Footnote omitted.

117

self-righteousness, that drove Wilson to his fatal choice. Perhaps this is true. He had not always been incapable of compromise; perhaps he would have yielded in the end if disease had not dethroned his reason.

These attempts to extenuate ignore the fact that there were fundamental and vital issues at stake in the controversy over the treaty—whether the United States would take leadership in the League of Nations without hesitations and reservations, or whether it would join the League grudgingly and with no promises to help maintain universal collective security. To Wilson the difference between what he fought for and what Lodge and the Republicans would agree to was the difference between the success or failure and the life or death of man's best hope for peace. This he had said on his western tour, at a time when his health and reasoning faculties were unimpaired. This he believed with his heart and soul. It is, therefore, possible, even probable, that Wilson would have acted as he did even had he not suffered his breakdown, for it was not in his nature to compromise away the principles in which he believed.

If this is true, then in this, the last and greatest effort of his life, Wilson spurned the role of statesman for what he must have thought was the nobler role of prophet. The truth is that the American people were not prepared in 1920 to assume the world leadership that Wilson offered them, and that the powers of the world were not yet ready to enforce the world-wide, universal system of collective security that the President had created.

Collective security failed in the portentous tests of the 1930's, not because the League's machinery was defective, but because the people of the world, not merely the American people alone, were unwilling to confront aggressors with the threat of war. As a result a second and more terrible world conflict came, as Wilson prophesied it would, and at its end the United States helped to build a new and different league of nations and took the kind of international leadership that Wilson had called for. But events of the past decade have not fully justified Wilson's confidence in international organization; the only really promising systems of collective security, the regional ones like NATO, have been of a kind that Wilson fervently denounced; and only the future can reveal whether his dream of a universal system can ever be made a reality.

And so it was Wilson the prophet, demanding greater commitment, sacrifice, and idealism than the people could give, who was defeated in 1920. It is also Wilson the prophet who survives in history, in the hopes and aspirations of mankind and in whatever ideals of international service that the American people still cherish. One thing is certain, now that men have the power to sear virtually the entire face of the earth: The prophet of 1919 was right in his larger vision; the challenge that he raised then is today no less real and no less urgent than it was in his own time.

Suggestions for Additional Reading

There are only two scholarly, thorough surveys of the League fight: Denna Frank Fleming, *The United States and the League of Nations* (New York, 1932); and Thomas A. Bailey, *Woodrow Wilson and the Peacemakers* (New York, 1947), published separately as *Woodrow Wilson and the Lost Peace* (New York, 1944) and *Woodrow Wilson and the Great Betrayal* (New York, 1945). In contrast to this dearth of comprehensive studies, there are scores of articles, monographs, and biographies that treat events and individuals as limited parts of the whole story. Before discussing some of these accounts, however, we should note a few of the outstanding sources.

A number of books of an autobiographical nature illuminate in particular the Senate and its role. *Crowded Hours* (New York, 1933) by Alice Roosevelt Longworth, Theodore Roosevelt's daughter, records some interesting conversations she had with certain irreconcilables. Royal W. France's *My Native Grounds* (New York, 1957) has helpful information about his brother, Senator Joseph Irwin France, an undeservedly obscure irreconcilable from Maryland. Another source for the anti-League Senators is George Wharton Pepper, *Philadelphia Lawyer, An Autobiography* (Philadelphia and New York, 1944). Oscar S. Strauss, *Under Four Administrations* (Boston, 1922) contains material on the proposals of the mild reservationists in August 1919. Vice President Thomas Marshall was in a unique position to observe the Senate, but his *Recollections* (Indianapolis, 1925), except for a few vivid character sketches, is of limited value. Two books that are useful for Republican party politics at this time are Nicholas Murray Butler, *Across*

the Busy Years (2 vols., New York, 1939–40) and *The Memoirs of Will Hays* (Garden City, N.Y., 1955). Books by senators themselves are few and disappointing. James E. Watson's *As I Knew Them* (Indianapolis, 1936) should not be relied on; the Indiana senator's memory of conversations was not always trustworthy. George Norris' autobiography, *Fighting Liberal* (New York, 1945), is much more reliable but not too revealing. Henry Fountain Ashurst, a Democrat who wanted Wilson to compromise with the Republicans, left behind a record of colorful observations, edited by G. F. Sparks and entitled, *A Many-Colored Toga: The Diary of Henry Fountain Ashurst* (Tuscon, Ariz., 1962). In a special category belongs Henry Cabot Lodge's *The Senate and the League of Nations* (New York, 1925). The book is primarily an attempt to explain and defend Lodge's actions. Lodge succeeds in showing the difficulties he faced and brilliantly overcame as majority leader of a party badly split on the League, but he also reveals his rankling ill will toward Wilson.

For sources focusing more directly on Wilson, one should begin with *The Public Papers of Woodrow Wilson*, edited by Ray S. Baker and William E. Dodd (6 vols., New York, 1925–27). They contain Wilson's speeches made on his "swing around the circle" as well as other speeches and his messages to Congress. Besides the autobiographical works already cited, a few others deserve mention. These include Edith Bolling Wilson, *My Memoir* (Indianapolis, 1939), which has the amusing story of the "smelling committee's" visit to Wilson's bedside after his stroke; Thomas W. Lamont, *Across World Frontiers* (New York, 1951);

David F. Houston, *Eight Years with Wilson's Cabinet, 1913–1920: with a Personal Estimate of the President* (2 vols., Garden City, N.Y., 1926); Ray Stannard Baker, *American Chronicle* (New York, 1945); Joseph Tumulty, *Woodrow Wilson as I Know Him* (Garden City, N.Y., 1921), important for certain letters and speeches of Wilson but unreliable in many ways; Josephus Daniels, *The Wilson Era* (2 vols., Chapel Hill, N.C., 1944–46). Charles Seymour (ed.), *The Intimate Papers of Colonel House* (4 vols., Boston and New York, 1926–28).

The secondary sources are diverse in nature. Biographies are useful, and some of the most useful are of persons outside government who were deeply involved in the fight. See in particular Philip C. Jessup, *Elihu Root* (2 vols., New York, 1938) and Claude G. Bowers, *Beveridge and the Progressive Era* (New York, 1932), both of which contain lengthy selections of the voluminous correspondence the two men carried on with senators. Also recommended are the following: Richard W. Leopold, *Elihu Root and the Conservative Tradition* (Boston, 1954); Henry F. Pringle, *The Life and Times of William Howard Taft* (2 vols., New York, 1939); Willis F. Johnson, *George Harvey, 'a Passionate Patriot'* (Boston and New York, 1929); George Harvey, *Henry Clay Frick* (New York, 1928); and Allan Nevins, *Henry White, Thirty Years of American Diplomacy* (New York, 1930).

Biographies of Wilson abound, but the "definitive" study by Arthur S. Link is still in progress. In five large and richly documented volumes, Link has carried the story into 1917. Until he reaches the League fight, one must rely on other completed works. Of these, the most recent is Arthur Clarence Walworth's *Woodrow Wilson* (Boston, 1965, second edition revised): his strongly sympathetic interpretation should be compared to the more critical John Morton Blum, *Woodrow Wilson and the Politics of Morality* (Boston and Toronto, 1956). Blum's *Joe Tumulty and the Wilson Era* (Boston, 1951) should also be mentioned. John A. Garraty, after his biography of Lodge, turned to Wilson and produced a highly readable interpretation, *Woodrow Wilson, A Great Life in Brief* (New York, 1956). For other books on Wilson, see the excellent article by Richard Watson, "Woodrow Wilson and His Interpreters, 1947–1957," *Mississippi Valley Historical Review* LXIV (September, 1957), 207–236.

Still to be written are biographies of several prominent senators of this period. Of those that do exist, the most helpful, apart from Garraty's work on Lodge, are Claudius O. Johnson, *Borah of Idaho* (New York, 1936) and Marian C. McKenna, *Borah* (Ann Arbor, Mich., 1961). Belle Case La Follette and Fola La Follette, *Robert M. La Follette* (2 vols., New York, 1953) is uncritical but the only detailed record of La Follette for these years. Sewell Thomas, *Silhouettes of Charles S. Thomas, Colorado Governor and United States Senator* (Caldwell, Idaho, 1959) is a superficial portrait but important because it quotes extensively from the senator's unpublished autobiography. A grossly inaccurate and partisan biography by Lee Meriwether, *Jim Reed "Senatorial Immortal"* (Webster Groves, Mo., 1948) should nevertheless be examined because of Meriwether's association with Reed at the time of the fight. Other biographies worth consulting include: Dewey W. Grantham, Jr., *Hoke Smith and the Politics of the New South* (Baton Rouge, La., 1958); George C. Osborn, *John Sharp Williams* (Baton Rouge, La., 1943); Rixey Smith and Norman Beasley, *Carter Glass* (New York, 1939); Fred L. Israel, *Nevada's Key Pittman* (Lincoln, Neb., 1963); and David Bryn-Jones, *Frank B. Kellogg* (New York, 1937). One should also see the study of Kellogg by Robert H. Ferrell in *American Secretaries of State and Their Diplomacy* (New York, 1963), XI. Not yet completed is the work by Richard Lowitt, the first volume of which is *George W. Norris, the Making of a Progressive, 1861–1912* (Syracuse, N.Y., 1963).

Studies of individual senators and of the Senate as a body are numerous. William E. Borah has been the subject of much investigation. In addition to the previously mentioned biographies, one can read with profit the book by John Chalmers Vinson, *William*

E. Borah and the Outlawry of War (Athens, Ga., 1957) ; and the articles by Claudius O. Johnson, "William E. Borah: The People's Choice," *Pacific Northwest Quarterly*, XLIV (January, 1953), 15–22; and Charles W. Toth, "Isolationism and the Emergence of Borah: An Appeal to American Tradition," *The Western Political Quarterly*, XIV (June, 1961), 555–568. Thomas F. Eagleton, *James A. Reed and the League of Nations* (Amherst, Mass., 1950) is brief, but does draw from some of Reed's personal correspondence. Ralph A. Stone, "Two Illinois Senators among the Irreconcilables," *Mississippi Valley Historical Review*, L (December, 1963), 443–465, deals with Medill McCormick and Lawrence Sherman. Dewey W. Grantham, Jr., "The Southern Senators and the League of Nations," *North Carolina Historical Review*, XXVI (April, 1949), 187–205, is the only regional study of its kind. Walter Johnson, "Senatorial Strategy, 1919–1920," *Antioch Review*, III (Winter, 1943), 512–529, views Lodge as working almost hand in glove with the irreconcilables to defeat the League. Rayford W. Logan, *The Senate and the Versailles Mandate System* (Washington, 1945) is excellent and far more inclusive than the title suggests.

Books and articles that consider special aspects of the story can be divided into several categories. On isolationism and collective security, see the collection of outstanding articles edited by Alexander DeConde, *Isolation and Security* (Durham, N.C., 1957) especially those by DeConde and Richard N. Current; the article by Roland N. Stromberg, "The Riddle of Collective Security, 1916–1920," in George L. Anderson (ed.), *Issues and Conflicts: Studies in Twentieth Century American Diplomacy* (Lawrence, Kan., 1959) ; and Robert E. Osgood, *Ideals and Self-interest in America's Foreign Relations: the Great Transformation of the Twentieth Century* (Chicago, 1953). Two articles that deal more directly with Wilson and collective security are Edward H. Buehrig, "Woodrow Wilson and Collective Security," in *Wilson's Foreign Policy in Perspective* (Bloomington, Ind., 1957) and Denna Frank Fleming, "Woodrow Wilson and Collective Security Today," *The Journal of Politics*, XVIII (November, 1956), 611–624. See also Herbert G. Nicholas, "Wilsonianism at Mid-Century," in *Centenaire Woodrow Wilson* (Geneva, 1956).

The elections of 1918 and 1920 were of great importance for the final outcome of the fight. Seward W. Livermore, "The Sectional Issue in the 1918 Congressional Elections," *Mississippi Valley Historical Review*, XXXV (June, 1948), 29–60, and Selig Adler, "The Congressional Election of 1918," *South Atlantic Quarterly*, XXVI (October, 1937), 447–465, analyze the meaning of the Republican victory of 1918; while Wesley M. Bagby, *The Road to Normalcy: The Presidential Campaign and Election of 1920* (Baltimore, 1962) is the most thorough study of the Harding sweep. Still worth reading for both elections is the book by Charles P. Howland, *Survey of American Foreign Relations, 1928* (New Haven, Conn., 1928).

Public opinion and the League has received surprisingly limited attention in view of the importance attached to it by so many at the time and since. The following articles, while useful, only indicate how much more needs to be done: James D. Startt, "Early Press Reaction to Wilson's League Proposal," *Journalism Quarterly*, XXXIX (Summer, 1962), 301–308; John A. Aman, "Views of Three Iowa Newspapers on the League of Nations," *Iowa Journal of History and Politics*, XXXIX (July, 1941), 227–285; and Mary Misaela Zacharewicz, "The Attitude of the Catholic Press toward the League of Nations," *Records of the American Catholic Historical Society of Philadelphia*, LXVII (1956), 3–30, 88–104; LXVIII (1957), 46–50.

On Wilson's "swing around the circle," see Dexter Perkins, "Woodrow Wilson's Tour," in Daniel Aaron (ed.), *America in Crisis* (New York, 1952), 245–265, and Gregg Phifer, "Woodrow Wilson's Swing Around The Circle in Defense of his League," *Florida State University Studies*, No. 23, *Woodrow Wilson Centennial Issue*, Victor S. Mamatey, ed., (Tallahassee, Fla. 1956), 65–102. The "Smelling Committee" visit is discussed in David H. Stratton, "President Wilson's Smelling Committee," *Colorado*

Quarterly, I (Autumn, 1956), 164–184. Kurt Wimer's article, "The League of Nations: A Victim of Executive-Legislative Rivalry," *Lock Haven Bulletin*, (February, 1960), 1–12, is good on the Constitutional issue. The failure of the Bipartisan Conference is the subject of the article by H. Maurice Darling, "Who Kept the United States out of the League of Nations," *Canadian Historical Review*, X (September, 1929), 196–211.

Books that take a broader view of the fight are: Ruhl J. Bartlett, *The League to Enforce Peace* (Chapel Hill, N.C., 1944); Louis A. R. Yates, *The United States and French Security, 1917–1921* (New York, 1957); and Alan Cranston, *The Killing of the Peace* (New York, 1945), a diatribe against Wilson's opponents. The biography by Warren Kuehl, *Hamilton Holt* (Gainesville, Fla., 1960) is very informative for the earlier part of the story.